P9-DOA-552

TRADE UNION DEMOCRACY
IN WESTERN EUROPE

A Publication of the
Institute of Industrial Relations
University of California

TRADE UNION DEMOCRACY IN WESTERN EUROPE

WALTER GALENSON

University of California Press
Berkeley and Los Angeles, 1962

University of California Press
Berkeley and Los Angeles, California
Cambridge University Press, London, England

© 1961 by The Regents of the University of California
Second Printing, 1962
Library of Congress Catalog Card Number: 61–6779

Manufactured in the United States of America

FOREWORD

Walter Galenson's study of *Trade Union Democracy in Western Europe* was conducted under the auspices of the Trade Union Study of the Center for the Study of Democratic Institutions. Supported by a generous grant from the Fund for the Republic, the Trade Union Study has been planned and directed by a committee under the chairmanship of Clark Kerr, President of the University of California. The other members of the committee are Benjamin Aaron, Walter Galenson, Paul Jacobs, Seymour M. Lipset, Philip Selznick, and W. Willard Wirtz. Four of the committee members (Kerr, Galenson, Lipset, and Selznick) are also members of the research staff of the Institute of Industrial Relations on the Berkeley campus of the University, while Benjamin Aaron is Director of the Institute of Industrial Relations on the Los Angeles campus. Thus the Institute has been closely associated with the Trade Union Study and is pleased to coöperate with the committee in sponsoring the publication of Professor Galenson's monograph.

Arthur M. Ross, Director

In this study, Walter Galenson has fulfilled a double purpose. On the one hand, he has written an excellent summary description of the structure of the European labor movement. That, in itself, is an accomplishment. On the other hand, he has made a very real contribution to the discussion of democracy and trade unionism in America. By helping us to see Europe, he helps us to see ourselves.

For example, it has been axiomatic among trade unionists in the United States that "dual unionism" is a serious evil. Indeed, there was an effort which lasted almost two decades which finally brought the AFL and the CIO together and produced the "No Raiding" agreement. But now, another question develops: has the worker lost some freedom of choice in that he no longer has the option to move to another International or another Federation? In the years since the merger of the AFL and the CIO, this issue has become more and more compelling.

Walter Galenson's study will not solve the American problem. But, by describing the variety of practices and attitudes in Europe, it makes a significant contribution to the discussion. In Belgium, Holland, and Austria there is dual unionism, and the labor movements of those countries accept this as a healthy, positive situation. In France and Italy, on the other hand, unions function in a different social context. This context reinforces the tendencies of weakness and factional political fragmentation in the labor movement.

Obviously, the fact that dual unionism works well in one country does not mean that it can be transplanted to the United States. As Galenson makes clear, the structure of unionism grows out of the economy, the social and political history, of a nation. In the United States, the Wagner Act made a momentous option for the concept of exclusive jurisdiction. This decision has now become integrated into our trade union life. It, along with a range of economic, historic, and social factors, has given real power to the traditional American rejection of dual unionism.

And yet understanding the European attitudes and practices does help to focus the question. It opens up a whole range of reference for the discussion which is taking place in America. Similarly with other problems. In Sweden and Britain, for instance, there is no real internal competition within the labor movement, yet this has not led to antidemocratic practices on a wide basis.

Or there is the question of the nonparticipation of the member in the affairs of his union. As this study makes plain, this is a problem in all the advanced nations. Yet the reason for it varies from country to country. In France and Italy, it is related to the weakness (really the absence) of strong locals; in Britain, it represents a change, part of the movement toward national bargaining; in Sweden, it may well be a function of the very success of the trade union movement. These facts do not carry with them some automatic conclusions of the problem of nonparticipation in America. Rather, they point out lines of investigation; they reveal possibilities which might not be so obvious to us.

Then, there are the white collar unions of Sweden. They are successful, organizationally independent of the blue collar unions, politically neutral, and they emphasize shop bargaining. Clearly, this is a phenomenon of importance for American unionists who are more and more faced with the possibility of organizing white collar and service workers. Walter Galenson's description is, of course, a summary one, yet even in broad outline the fact of white collar unionism in Sweden is tremendously relevant to the American labor movement today.

The examples could be multiplied many times over, but the main point should be obvious.

We of the Trade Union Study of the Center for the Study of Democratic Institutions have concentrated upon the problem of freedom in American unions. This study by Walter Galenson is a valuable addition to the literature of scholarship, an extremely useful survey of European trade union structures. But at every point it is also, at least by implication, a contribution to the discussion of the labor movement in America. We cannot become "visitors from Mars" so as to see our institutions without any assumptions or bias. We can, however, become visitors to other nations, to other labor movements, and in the doing we can gain a new angle of vision upon the issue of democracy in our industrialized society. This Walter Galenson helps us to do, and we are in his debt.

Clark Kerr

ACKNOWLEDGMENTS

This study is based largely upon interviews conducted in Europe during the spring and summer of 1959. It does not pretend to be encyclopedic. On the contrary, it covers only those aspects of the subject which are of greatest current interest either in Europe or in the United States. A thorough monographic treatment would require years—not months—of investigation and analysis.

A great many persons gave generously of their time and advice, too numerous to mention here. However, I must at least acknowledge the assistance of those who went to the trouble of scheduling interviews for me; without their help it would have been impossible to utilize the limited time at my disposal at all effectively. They are: Hugh Clegg, Nuffield College, Oxford University; Allan Flanders, Institute of Statistics, Oxford University; Henning Friis, Director, the Danish National Institute of Social Research; Dr. Gino Guigni, Institute of Industrial Reconstruction, Rome; Professor Charles A. Gulick, University of California, Berkeley;

Daniel Horowitz, Labor Attaché, United States Embassy, Paris; Haakon Lie, General Secretary, Norwegian Labor party; Professor Val R. Lorwin, University of Oregon; Dr. Gustavo Malan, Director, European Institute for Economic Studies, Turin; Professor Jan Pen, University of Groningen; Gösta Rehn, Economist, Swedish Federation of Labor; Dr. Philip Rieger, Vienna Chamber of Labor; and Professor A. J. Rüter, Director, International Institute of Social History, Amsterdam.

It is one of the purposes of the Fund for the Republic, which sponsored this study, to stimulate discussion of public issues. I have tried to do my part by eschewing academic detachment and expressing my own opinion whenever it seemed appropriate. But it would be the height of ingratitude to incriminate those who were kind enough to help me, so that it is necessary to append the customary avowal of sole responsibility for all the views that appear in the following pages.

W. G.

CONTENTS

INTRODUCTION

In spite of the appearances of geography, Western Europe is far from a homogeneous area. There are striking differences among the nations which comprise it both in politics and economics. The variation is certainly not so great as between the capitalist and communist worlds, or between developed and undeveloped nations, but it is substantial enough to provide material for interesting contrasts.

Specifically as to the institutions of the labor market, the nine countries which we will consider run the gamut from a pre-Wagner Act type of antiunionism to streamlined systems of collective bargaining. In the former, the unions are engrossed in a struggle to survive. Elsewhere, they have attained an impregnable status, and are almost governmental bodies functionally.

To be sure, certain basic problems are found wherever one goes. Some of these relate to organizational considerations: for example, what is the proper balance between strong leadership and rank and file participation in union affairs? Or, what is the appropriate division of authority among the federation, the national union, and the local union? Other problems, and it is these with which we will be mainly concerned, center around the place of an individual in an organization. What protection should be accorded to dissident minorities? What shall be done with the convinced nonunion man in a union world? It should not surprise anyone, however, that there is no uniformity in the intensity of interest which these and similar questions arouse. Where a union is fighting for its life, there is apt to be little concern with the niceties of democratic procedure. Individual rights are more likely to be sacrificed to the "common good" than when the organization is secure from outside attack. If there is one lesson to be learned from the European experience, it is that union security, in the broader sense, is a necessary (though not sufficient) condition for internal democracy.

The nine countries which comprise our sample can be divided into three major groups, in terms of our interests. Italy and France clearly belong together, for despite the tremendous differences in the histories of the two nations, the end result for trade unionism is much the same. We can put Belgium, Holland, and Austria into a second group. The last named has some unique characteristics, but it is close enough to the others to warrant common analysis. Our final category includes Great Britain and the Scandinavian nations, which are closest to the United States model. After considering each group in turn, I shall attempt to generalize from the similarities and contrasts that appear.

CHAPTER I. THE WEAKNESS OF RIVAL UNIONISM: ITALY AND FRANCE

The overwhelming impression that confronts the observer of the Italian and French labor movements is their impotence. This fact overshadows all else, and is reflected at every turn. We do not have sufficient space to look into history for an explanation of how the present state of affairs came to be; the interested reader is urged to explore the past for himself.[1] We will limit ourselves to defining the weakness and examining its implications.

---

[1] This can be done easily and conveniently for France, via the excellent monograph by Val R. Lorwin, *The French Labor Movement* (Cambridge: Harvard University Press, 1954). The problem is much more difficult to solve for Italy, even if one is willing to tackle works in Italian. To avoid a long bibliographical footnote, the reader is referred to Joseph La Palombara, *The Italian Labor Movement* (Ithaca: Cornell University Press, 1957), where he will find material on recent developments and an adequate bibliography.

UNION MEMBERSHIP

The most obvious index of trade union strength—or weakness—is the degree of organization that has been achieved. Unfortunately, this is not an easy quantity to determine for Italy and France. Everyone has his own estimate of Italian union membership, and rarely is there any coincidence among the estimates. La Palombara, in 1957, stated that "not many more than six million of Italy's workers (30 per cent of the labor force) are organized."[2] A well-informed Italian student of labor affairs gave me an estimate of slightly more than five million in 1959, and this figure, as an outside limit, is more consistent with the disaggregated components of the total.

Membership is shared among four separate, independent, and bitterly hostile labor federations. The largest is the Communist-controlled *Confederazione Generale Italiana del Lavoro* (CGIL), which, although it claims four million adherents, is probably closer to two and a half million. Second, with something less than two million members, is the Catholic-supported *Confederazione Italiana Sindicati Lavoratori* (CISL). Far behind are the Socialist-oriented *Unione Italiana del Lavoro* (UIL), which has fallen to about 200,000 members, and CISNAL, a neo-fascist organization of about 100,000. There are also a number of independent unions, particularly among civil servants and teachers.[3]

Now, a total union membership of five million, or even four million, out of a labor force of some twenty million is quite respectable as these things go in the world today. The trouble is that many of these members have only a nominal attachment to their unions. In 1956, for example, only between 30 and 40 per cent of dues owed the three major federations were actually paid.[4] A CISL official in Turin, one of the strongholds of Italian unionism, asserted recently that between 40 and 45 per cent of his membership were paying dues of 2,000 lire (about $3.00) a year regularly,

---

[2] La Palombara, *op. cit.*, p. 109. The same figure is given by Maurice F. Neufeld, "The Italian Labor Movement in 1956," *The Annals of the American Academy*, Volume 310 (March, 1957), p. 75.

[3] CISL claimed a membership of 2.3 million at the end of 1958, and put the membership of its competitors as follows: CGIL, 2.3 million; UIL, 552,000; CISNAL, 100,000. These figures must be taken with a grain of salt, since CISL obviously has a stake in inflating its own membership claims and denigrating its rivals. It is interesting to note, however, that the total membership for all unions, as stated by CISL, is not much more than 5 million. See CISL, *Italian Labor Documents*, November 15, 1959.

[4] Neufeld, *op. cit.*, p.75.

surely not a spectacular claim. Although the state of Italian trade union finances is a closely guarded secret, it is generally understood that none of the federations is self-supporting. CGIL is believed to receive subsidies from the Communist party, CISL from the American labor movement, and the neo-fascist union from employers. UIL officials are willing to admit that very few within their dwindling ranks pay the dues of 100 lire a month, and that they are subsisting largely on assistance from the international labor movement.

When one asks why the Italian worker does not join a union, unemployment is almost invariably cited as the primary cause. Precisely how much unemployment there is in Italy is a matter of some dispute. Like union membership, it is not always easy to define. Some put it as high as 20 per cent of the labor force, but half that figure appears to be a more reasonable estimate. Even at 10 per cent, however, holding his job is a critical matter for the worker, for he may not be able to get another. Most grievances and strikes are over the issue of discharge rather than wages. Workers are often afraid to become union members lest they offend their employers, for victimization of active unionists is not unknown. On occasion, workers even abstain conspicuously from voting in secret elections for shop committees, lest their presence at the polls be construed as support for the Communist slate. There are other reasons, as we shall see, but the importance of structural unemployment as a determinant of worker and employer behavior cannot be overemphasized.

The French unions are in much the same boat as the Italian. Michel Collinet, a close student of French labor, estimates current union membership as follows: the communist *Confédération Générale du Travail* (CGT), 1.0 to 1.2 million; the Catholic *Confédération Française des Travailleurs Chrétiens* (CFTC), 500,000; and the socialist-inclined *Force Ouvrière* (FO), 500,000. Even with independent groups counted in, the grand total is well below three million. And as in Italy, members pay dues, on the average, for only two or three months a year, although annual dues are only about 2,000 francs ($4.00).

COLLECTIVE BARGAINING

The prevailing system of collective bargaining[5] both reflects and

---

[5] For a good treatment of this subject, see Adolf Sturmthal, ed., *Contemporary Collective Bargaining in Seven Countries* (Ithaca: Cornell University Press, 1957).

contributes to trade union weakness. Nearly all Italian agreements are negotiated on an industry-wide basis between associations of employers and national unions. In fact, for many industries, the federations of labor determine policy and even conduct negotiations. On some occasions, bargaining has been conducted with all the federations acting jointly, and at other times there have been separate negotiations with smaller groups. The final result is generally a national industrial agreement that is uniform for all unions and all firms in the industry.

Each federation has an interest in demonstrating that it alone is capable of producing economic gains for industrial workers, and there is constant jockeying for position, with inevitable loss of over-all union power. Individual plant, local, and even regional collective agreements are almost entirely lacking. "The metal-mechanical unions of the competing labor federations, considered the strongest in the country, have succeeded in organizing less than 40 per cent of the workers under their jurisdiction. Moreover, eight years elapsed before the parties to this key contract for all labor groups throughout the country could bring their 1948 partial agreements to conclusion in 1956. So fared collective bargaining in the most powerful of Italy's category federations."[6]

The situation in France is somewhat more complicated, though the end result is the same. There are local agreements (many fewer relatively than in the United States) as well as national agreements, but in effect, all major economic dcisions are made at the top, with the government playing a major role through determination of minimum occupational wages for all industry, and key bargains in the substantial nationalized sector. Here again, intense interunion rivalry serves to diminish the collective bargaining power of labor. To quote Adolf Sturmthal: "Collective bargaining still plays a secondary role in regulating industrial relations in France. The State, on the one hand, and the more or less unilateral decision of the employer, play a more significant part than bargaining between employer and unions."[7] The inevitable result, in both France and Italy, is emphasis upon political rather than economic action, upon left wing political parties

---

[6] Maurice F. Neufeld, "The Inevitability of Political Unionism in Underdeveloped Countries," *Industrial and Labor Relations Review,* Vol. 13 (April, 1960), p. 385.

[7] Sturmthal, *op. cit.,* p. 165.

rather than trade unions, as the means of diverting a greater proportion of the national income to workers.

LOCAL ORGANIZATION

Membership is not the only index of union strength. Perhaps of even greater significance, particularly with the problem of union democracy in mind, is the solidity of local organization. And here the Italian and French labor movements are in dire straits indeed. Instead of plant locals, one finds a hodgepodge of institutional devices which, though seemingly democratic in conception, actually stifle the growth of genuine trade unionism, and play into the hands of the antilabor employer.

The chief representative body of workers in the Italian factory is the grievance committee (*commissione interna*).[8] Its members are elected annually on the basis of slates proposed by affiliates of the national labor federations. However, one need not be a union member to vote; there is universal suffrage among all workers and employees in the plant. The consequence of union pluralism is that most grievance committees are composed of partisans of the different labor groups, many of them antipathetic to one another. Grievance committee elections are widely regarded as the best available index of the relative strength of the unions, and are followed almost as closely as political elections. Election campaigns are hard fought, and often entail the expenditure of substantial amounts of money, which the unions can ill afford. But to fall behind one's competitor, even by a fraction of a percentage point, is to court disaster.

The grievance committee is in effect the counterpart of the local union in the United States. It handles individual complaints, supervises the execution of the national collective agreement, and deals with management on plant rules, piece rates, working hours, and health and welfare activities. This institution has a long history in Italy, so that the worker instinctively looks to it, rather than to the trade union, for assistance in securing redress of real or fancied wrongs.

At first encounter, the grievance committee may impress one as an ideal arrangement. When the Wagner Act was being debated

---

[8] For a detailed study of how such bodies operate, see Maurice F. Neufeld, *Labor Unions and National Politics in Italian Industrial Plants*, (Ithaca: Cornell University Press, 1954).

5

in the United States in 1934, there were many who favored proportional representation rather than exclusive majority representation; it was only the adamant opposition of the American Federation of Labor which prevented this scheme from being written into federal law. The whole issue of compulsory unionism is effectively bypassed; workers are afforded a regular opportunity to designate their representatives by secret ballot; and the committee that is elected reflects every shade of opinion within the shop. For example, the following results were obtained at the 1958 grievance committee election at the Turin Fiat works, one of the most critical elections in all Italy (the figures are rounded):

Eligible to vote	65,000
CGIL	14,400
CISL	7,500
UIL	16,000
CISNAL (neo-fascist)	1,300
LLD (independent)	17,750
Invalid ballots	3,000
Not voting	5,050

In this much-discussed election, the LLD (Free Democratic Workers), a breakaway group from CISL, secured the largest number of votes, and consequently the largest representation on the grievance committee. Its president, Edoardo Arrighi, had been expelled from CISL for what he alleges was a campaign to strengthen internal democracy, although his opponents claim that he is an opportunist in league with management. Whatever the truth may be, it proved possible for a new group to win the leading position on the grievance committee over the strenuous opposition of entrenched interests.[9]

The fundamental defect of the grievance committee pattern of proportional representation is that it deprives the union of contact with the individual and greatly lessens worker interest in unionism. At the same time, it cannot afford that degree of protection of worker interests against employers which can come only from

----

[9] In the April, 1960, elections, with 73,000 workers voting, the Communist-dominated CGIL polled 21.8 per cent of the votes, a slight advance over their 1959 position. The Socialist UIL jumped into a commanding position with 27.5 per cent of all the votes, compared with only 16.5 per cent in 1959. CISL, CISNAL, and the independent LLD experienced a decline in their voting strength. *New York Times,* April 8, 1960, p. 3.

organizations extending beyond a single plant or company. An inside organization, particularly when split up among competing factions, lends itself to employer manipulation, if not control.

The problem that faces Italian unions is that despite these drawbacks, of which they are painfully aware, the grievance committee system cannot be attacked directly: it provides a central rallying point, and all workers, regardless of ideology, are loyal to it. A particular difficulty for the non-Communist unions is that the CGIL, as the dominant federation, controls a majority of the members on many grievance committees, and is able to exploit its position to the disadvantage of the others, often forcing them to follow its lead. After the Hungarian revolution of 1956, Communist strength in grievance committee elections declined, but in the past year it has been on the upgrade once more for the following reasons. A decreasing proportion of the workers has been voting, so that loyal CGIL adherents can make their weight better felt. In 1958, CISL and UIL opposed CGIL with the slogan, "Give us a year to show what we can do." The year went by, few gains were forthcoming, and the workers are swinging back to the more extreme organization. The CGIL has made a conscious effort to improve communications with individual workers. In some shops, CGIL members have for the first time been permitted to elect the CGIL slate, rather than having it done from above.

The frequency of balloting for grievance committees means that electioneering never stops. There is a great deal of demagogism, with the unions regularly making promises they cannot hope to fulfill. Some grievance committees are able to subordinate their factional interests to work in unity for the common interests of their constituents, but with another election always around the corner, union partisans must be alert for the main chance. CISL has recently taken some cautious steps toward advocacy of a reduced role for the grievance committee,[10] but against this is the combined influence of the Communists and the employers, the latter because they are not anxious to have local unions directly in their plants. There is also a natural conservatism on the part of

---

[10] For example, Claudio Cruciani, Secretary of CISL, recently wrote: "In the light of its experiences, the C.I.S.L. does not regard the Shop Stewards' Committee with enthusiasm, and looks upon it as a somewhat equivocal instrument of workers' representation which often prevents the union from entering a firm, thereby hindering factory-level negotiation. . . . This line of policy has led us to the deliberate rejection of any attempt at legal recognition of the bodies which represent the workers in the factories." CISL, *Italian Labor Documents*, No. 17, 1960.

the workers, fearful of weakening the one local institution to which they can now turn with their problems. All in all, the outlook for change is not bright.

The French situation is even more complicated. The problem there is not one, but a multiplicity of grievance channels, all divorced from formal trade union structure. The two main representative bodies at the local level are the shop stewards' committee (*délégués du personnel*) and the enterprise committee (*comité d'enterprise*). In theory, the former has a legal right to handle local bargaining matters, whereas the latter is supposed to confine itself to consultation with management on welfare questions, dismissals, layoffs, and the general economic policies of the firm. As a practical matter, there is often a blurring of functional lines between the two. In some plants the enterprise committees have large budgets for operating canteens and other social services, so that they have much patronage to dispense, an attractive feature for trade unions with meager financial resources of their own. The Communist party, through the CGT, has been particularly adept at milking these bodies to help support its activities.

Both the shop stewards' and enterprise committees are elected annually through proportional representation, on the basis of universal franchise without any condition as to union membership. On the first ballot, only unions recognized as "representative" by the government can present lists of candidates, but if less than half the eligible workers vote, anyone may run on the second ballot. In almost every instance the committees are split among partisans of the major labor federations. Moreover, since union membership is so low, workers in effect have to choose from among candidates selected by small groups of active union members. In the Renault automobile plant at Boulogne-Billancourt, for example, where 35,000 are employed, the CGT has 3,000 members, CFTC about 400, and FO about 200; yet it is these nuclei who designate the union slates.[11]

Because there is some local organization in the larger French plants, it is not unusual to find a separate local union for each of the major federations. However, even where they exist, the locals

---

11 These figures were given to me by Michel Collinet. For a good study of Renault shop organization, see André Tiano, Michel Rocard, and Hubert Lesire-Ogrel, *Expériences Francaises d'Action Syndicale Ouvrière*, (Paris: Les Éditions Ouvrières, 1956).

have few functions beyond providing guidance to their members on the stewards' and enterprise committees. As in Italy, the unions cannot openly attack the committee system, and must play the game actively to keep their election percentages from slipping. As to the worker, Lorwin has summed up his situation as follows:

. . . he finds the functions, like the personnel, of stewardship, plant committees, and union overlapping and blurring into each other. Often he hardly distinguishes among them. If he has any contact with the union branch or local, it is not usually in a function of on-the-job protection for him. The multiplicity of grievance channels dilutes his potential loyalty to the union organization, as distinct from the peripheral attachment of periodic shop votes or the sporadic manifestation of strikes.[12]

UNION STRUCTURE AND GOVERNMENT

The Italian and French unions are fully aware of the gap at the base of their structural pyramids, and within recent years have attempted to close it. In 1955, the Italian CISL began to set up local unions, followed shortly by CGIL, but neither campaign can be accounted a success. In Bologna, a city of some 400,000, not a single local union is functioning. In Turin, there are twenty CGIL and forty CISL locals, but none has any real power or any contact with employers. However, each union does have its own activist group in the factory. Here are the real spark plugs of trade unionism: the unpaid volunteers who distribute union literature and provide the only link between the union and the workers. On the CGIL side, these are likely to be Communist party members; on the CISL side, ardent Catholics.

The most important echelon in Italian union structure, apart from the federation at the very top, is the provincial chamber of labor. In many parts of the country it keeps the embers of unionism going. The chambers sometimes negotiate with employers on those grievances of their members which cannot be adjusted by the plant grievance committees; but, generally speaking, they do not have any extensive collective bargaining functions. The larger chambers are sectionalized by industry, with each section belonging to the national union exercising jurisdiction over the industry. However, it is to the chamber, not to the national union, that

---

12 Lorwin, *op. cit.*, p. 276.

workers tend to look for assistance. This is in sharp contrast to the United States, where the regional central trades councils are completely subordinate to the national unions.

The Turin CGIL Chamber of Labor, the largest of all the chambers with the exception of that in Milan, has about fifty employees, twenty of whom work directly for the chamber, the rest for national unions. The rival CISL chamber is almost equal in size. The chambers provide meeting places for local union groups, carry on educational and organizational work, and perform some of the other service functions that would normally belong to the nonexistent local unions. One of the main reasons for their importance, however, is the deep involvement of Italian unions in politics. For political effectiveness, it is important to have an adequate horizontal organizational structure.

Compared with the chambers of labor, the national unions are mostly weak and impoverished.[13] Here is the greatest contrast with the United States and the other European countries in our study, for in these countries the wealth and power of the labor movement tend to be concentrated in the national union. Few Italian unions are able to maintain an adequate network of provincial branches. The optimum is a few part-time organizers in the larger industrial centers, attached to the chambers of labor. The CISL Food Industry Union, one of the thirty-three national industrial unions in the federation, is a case in point. With 20,000 members in a 250,000-worker jurisdiction (the corresponding CGIL union has 30,000 members), its national office consists of two full-time officers and a typist. Liaison with regional bodies is difficult to maintain because of staff limitations. When new collective agreements are being negotiated, suggestions are solicited from the part-time or volunteer regional officers of the union. The letters sent out are usually answered by the chambers of labor, which have little contact with individual food plants.

The statutes of most unions provide for democratic control, but in fact very little rank and file activity is in evidence. Until a few years ago, delegates to various representative assemblies in the Turin CGIL were elected by the membership, the elections being held in cafés near the larger plants. Today the unions are so weak that formal elections are rare and delegates are simply designated

---

[13] There are some exceptions, of course. For example, the CISL national union in the metal trades is fairly well financed and consequently enjoys a considerable degree of autonomy.

by union activists. The CISL Food Industry Union holds a national congress every two or three years, finances permitting, but the union is run by a twenty-man executive board which meets several times a year. General secretaries of national unions must stand for reëlection at each congress, but there is almost no turnover. There is somewhat more change in provincial leadership—perhaps 20 per cent from congress to congress—but this is true because provincial salaries are so low as to make the positions undesirable if industrial jobs are available. In 1959, 80,000 lire a month (about $125.00) was the maximum salary of a provincial official, 50,000 to 60,000 lire, about what a skilled worker can earn, being more common. National salaries are somewhat better, but not strikingly so. The general secretary of a national union may earn enough to afford a small automobile, though one told me that his family holds a discussion every month on whether or not they can afford to attend a movie.

Real power in the Italian labor movement is vested in the federation. Although collective agreements are normally industry-wide in scope, federation secretaries do much of the actual bargaining.[14] National unions are subsidized by the federation, rather than the more normal reverse pattern. This circumstance makes for a highly centralized labor movement, with little in the way of membership participation. There are no general membership meetings, no referenda on agreements, no strike votes, and no elections in any real sense. A good part of this springs from the reluctance of the Italian worker to pay dues, but lack of contact with the union reinforces this reluctance in turn.

These observations apply, though with somewhat lesser force, to France. The CGT is controlled, from top to bottom, by the Communist party. Power is more decentralized within the Catholic CFTC and the socialist FO, and more decisions are made locally. French national unions are somewhat better organized than their Italian counterparts, but they are a far cry from the autonomous national unions of Britain and the United States. By the same token, French regional organization is weaker than that in Italy, the French departmental confederation being but a feeble echo of the Italian chamber of labor.

---

[14] Very recently, CISL has attempted to inaugurate more factory-level bargaining, and to get into such matters as local wage structure, hiring policy, industrial training, social insurance, and work safety. To what extent this policy will prove successful remains to be seen.

Formally, French union constitutions are quite democratic. Officers are paid moderate salaries, and are required to stand for reëlection periodically. Policies are laid down by representative bodies, which usually meet on schedule. But in the CGT, democratic forms are nullified by the omnipresent Communist organizer, and factionalism in CFTC and FO reflects more the weakness of these federations than any vigorous internal life. Far from being oppressed by a union bureaucracy, the French worker is badly in need of much more substantially built organizations to represent his economic interests. But as long as he persists in his traditional willingness to die on the barricades but to refuse to pay his union dues,[15] he is not likely to get them.

UNIONS AND POLITICS

Trade unionism in Italy and France is fully as political as economic in character. This has been said many times, but it cannot be overemphasized. Cause and effect are inextricably intertwined when one attempts to determine why this is true. Slow and imperfect economic development frustrated workers in their efforts to improve their living standards through collective bargaining, and, like workers everywhere who have been faced with this obstacle, they turned to politics for a quick and easy solution. Once politicized, the unions were too important to their allied political parties to permit their evolution into more neutral economic organizations. Political division contributed to economic weakness, and tended in turn to increase reliance on political methods.

It is a commonplace in Italy that, above all, workers want unity in the labor movement. The grievance committees owe their strength to the fact that they are unified. But no one is able to see any end to the warfare that divides the trade union federations. Each federation insists that it is the only true representative of working class interests and is not prepared to make any concessions in the quest for unity, not even in the face of the common opponent, the employer.

The dominant CGIL, though controlled by the Communist party in the final analysis, has a substantial internal minority in

---

[15] Professor Lorwin observed to me recently that even this hallowed tradition may have gone the way of so many other traditions under the Fifth Republic.

the adherents of the Nenni Socialist party. There is an unwritten agreement between the two groups on the allocation of jobs, the typical pattern being for the Communists to have the secretary-ship, and the Socialists the vice-secretaryship, at each administrative level. There is also an understanding that neither party is to dominate the provincial chambers of labor. The Communists are no longer able to use the CGIL for crude political purposes, as they once did, lest they drive the increasingly independent Socialists away. The latter, for example, were able to keep the CGIL from coming out in opposition to the establishment of the Common Market, which was the line of the Communist party. The CGIL has turned to bread-and-butter issues, and is eschewing such former abstractions as the breakup of business monopoly, once a prime objective. The Socialists, however, are equally fearful of a split in the CGIL which would probably leave them with a small minority of the members. This rather uneasy alliance bids fair to continue since both parties have little to gain and much to lose from a split.

Although it has taken pains to assert its political neutrality, CISL is closely identified in the public mind with the governing Christian Democratic party. The 1959 CISL Congress called for "an increasingly independent character on the part of the union movement as regards the political parties," and "reaffirmation of the will to combat all conditioning of trade union policy by political party interests." Nonetheless, it will be difficult to convince Italian workers that CISL is in fact independent of party politics. There is a considerable degree of personal interlocking between unions and party, but there are no formal ties. About thirty CISL officials are Christian Democratic members of parliament. (CGIL has about forty deputies belonging to the Communist and Socialist parties.) The UIL, divided between the Social Democratic and the Republican parties, is subject to less political influence because of the weakness of these two parties, but it is not a proponent of union neutrality.

In sum, Italian trade unionism is firmly wedded to political action, if for no other reason than that its power is much greater in this sphere than in the use of economic weapons. Each faction has its own dreams of unity, with itself as the leading partner: CISL sees itself absorbing UIL and gaining a monopoly of anti-Communist unionism; UIL hangs on to the hope that it may become a bridge between CISL and the Socialist wing of CGIL; the

13

Nenni Socialists conceive it to be their task to bore from within the CGIL, challenging the Communists on specific issues, and trade-unionizing the trade unions. At present, none of these dreams seems close to realization.

Of the French trade unions, Lorwin has written: "The unions in France are less instruments of collective bargaining than of political action. Workers have joined unions in great part as a 'reflex' of class consciousness rather than as a move for job control."[16] In spite of the political cataclysm that has overtaken France, this generalization still holds true, though the role that trade unions are destined to play in the new order is not yet clear.

French unions have operated on the theory that substantial gains can be made only in periods of crisis. Between crises they negotiate rather hopelessly. There is a deep-seated conviction that only through radical political and economic change can workers hope to achieve any real improvement in their lot. The result is that all unions have tended to remain at a distance from the daily, humdrum problems that workers have in dealing with their employers. A heroic tradition and collective bargaining do not go well together.

As far as one can judge, the Communist CGT still retains the loyalty of a majority of French trade unionists. Ever since the war, this union has been an instrument of Communist policy rather than a collective bargaining agency. Until a few years ago it managed to defeat its own purposes by a series of disastrous political strikes, but recently more cautious tactics have been adopted.

The CFTC, though Catholic in inspiration, has been less closely identified with Catholic political groups than the Italian CISL. The upsurge of Gaullism has left it without any real political base, and some of its left-wing members have become identified with the Mendès-France tendency. Its strength lies in the fact that it is the only real alternative to Communist unionism and that it has been willing to join the CGT on specific economic issues, thus avoiding the fatal charge, for France, of being lacking in militancy. FO, a vaguely socialist body with more influence among white collar workers and civil servants than among factory employees, has become a relatively minor factor in the union picture. More than the CFTC, it feels itself in direct competition with

---

[16] Lorwin, *op. cit.*, p. 278.

CGT for members, and most of its national unions have been less willing to collaborate with the CGT in general economic actions.

French and Italian trade unionism has more resemblance to labor organization in underdeveloped countries than in advanced industrial nations. There is lack of organization at the local level; membership is relatively small and not inured to the payment of dues; control is from the top, with little membership participation; and the method of political action is favored over collective bargaining. Political ideology, rather than economic service, is the binding agent between worker and union.

The labor market institutions that have developed since the war confirm these tendencies. Grievance committees, shop stewards' committees, enterprise committees provide a substitute, however inadequate, for local unions, and inhibit the growth of grass-roots unionism. Industry- and nation-wide collective bargaining reinforce centralization of function. Reliance on what the Webbs termed the method of legal enactment rather than collective bargaining, born of economic weakness, deprives the union of what is its chief *raison d'être* in other countries.

The French or Italian worker has an abundance of choice among unions, and is under no compulsion whatsoever to join any union. He can choose on the basis of politics or religion, and leave whenever it suits his fancy. His only problem is to find an organization capable of representing his interests in an effective manner. Given union weakness, it is small wonder that no one is particularly concerned about the whole range of problems subsumed under the concept of union democracy. Union officers consider themselves quite fortunate if there is a devoted group of activists willing to keep the organization alive.

A large measure of responsibility for this state of affairs rests with employers. They have taken advantage of union rivalry, and of Communist control of the largest federations to avoid collective relationships with their employees. Their policy has been to keep the unions out of the shop, to share out enough of their economic gains to keep workers from violent protest, and (in Italy) to nip revolt in the bud by the threat of unemployment.

It may be that this policy will prove successful. Certainly, if the goal of employer policy is to weaken unionism, the French and Italians have developed a model for employers of other countries. But in the long run, this policy is fraught with danger to the stability of the democratic state itself. The stock-in-trade of the Communist party is the intransigence of employers. It is not fundamentally a matter of wages, for real wages have moved up steadily, though probably not so rapidly as they would have with American-style unionism. It is more a question of industrial democracy, of the dignity of the individual employee, of his sense of impotence in the face of employer power. Perhaps the workers are too cowed to engage in any extremist political adventures, but they seem to have lost their ardor for defending democracy.

The diagnosis of what is wrong with the labor movements in these countries is not too difficult to make, but prescribing a cure is a different matter. French and Italian industrialists are no more likely to yield any part of their authority voluntarily than were their American colleagues twenty-five years ago. There is nothing on the horizon to indicate that government will force them to do so. The unions are losing ground, and it is probably fair to say that they are weaker than at any time since the end of the war. Optimists hope that rising living standards and fuller employment may lead to a dampening of employer-worker animosities and a greater accommodation between the organizations representing the two groups. This would entail depoliticizing of the unions and their concentration on collective bargaining. Employers will have to be willing to share some of the managerial prerogatives with the unions. But optimists are not too easily found. Pessimism is easier to justify by recent events; if the pessimists are borne out, democracy is in for some very severe tests in these two major areas of Western Europe.

CHAPTER II. THE STRENGTH OF RIVAL UNIONISM: BELGIUM, HOLLAND, AND AUSTRIA

Competition among unions need not have disastrous results either for workers or for the community. Given certain conditions, competition may bring economic benefits at least equal to those obtained when a single labor federation holds sway, and may yield an additional bonus in terms of augmented freedom of choice for the worker. The postwar experience of three small nations, Belgium, Holland, and Austria, provides a case study in union competition that deserves more attention than it has received.[1]

Those familiar with the Austrian scene will undoubtedly be

---

[1] There are as yet no full length treatises in English dealing with the postwar labor problems of any of these countries. The best articles are the following: Bert Zoeteweij, "National Wage Policy: the Experience of the Netherlands," *International Labour Review,* Vol. 71 (February, 1955), p. 1; P. S. Pels, "The Development of Collective Employment Agreements in the Netherlands," in Adolf Sturmthal, ed., *Contemporary Collective Bargaining in Seven Countries*

puzzled by the inclusion of that country in the rival union category, for there is a single, powerful federation of labor. As we will show, however, beneath the façade of unity there is multiple unionism almost as significant, in terms of individual choice, as in the other two countries.

UNION MEMBERSHIP

As in France and Italy, workers are confronted with a choice of unions in Belgium, Holland, and, in a real sense, in Austria. But there, any resemblance between the two groups ends. Communist-dominated unionism has practically disappeared in Belgium and Holland, and it is only a minor factor in Austria. Religious considerations loom larger. The traditional democratic socialism of Western Europe, though its relative strength has been declining since the war, is still the senior partner in the trade union movement, and not the dwindling third force that it has become in France and Italy.

Before the war, the *Confédération Générale du Travail de Belgique,* with more than 500,000 members, was the standard trade union body of Belgium. Its chief competitor, the *Confédération des Syndicats Chrétiens* (CSC), with about 300,000 members, was part of a network of social organizations sponsored by the Catholic Church. A smaller body, the *Central Générale du Syndicats Liberaux,* under Liberal party influence, consisted mainly of white collar employees.

During the German occupation, the resistance movement included several new labor groups. In April, 1945, these bodies joined with the old Socialist federation to form a new *Fédération Générale du Travail de Belgique* (FGTB), but as a concession to the non-Socialists, the federation was obliged to sever its formal ties with the Belgian Socialist party. However, the Catholic CSC and the liberal unions refused to join the new coalition, and the pattern of pluralism in the labor movement was confirmed.

At present, the FGTB and the CSC are of almost equal strength, with roughly 700,000 members each. The liberal federation is much smaller, and its role among wage earners is negligible. The

(Ithaca: Cornell University Press, 1957); B. C. Roberts, *National Wages Policy in War and Peace* (London: 1958), pp. 118–134; Charles A. Gulick, "Austrian Labor's Bid for Power," *Industrial and Labor Relations Review,* Vol. 12 (October, 1958), 35.

FGTB has somewhat more power than the CSC, in spite of equality of membership, because it is more concentrated in heavy industry and larger plants and has a greater following among unorganized workers. The CSC is more important in textiles, building construction, and white collar trades. About two-thirds of potential trade union members are organized, and some of the unorganized are special foreign labor groups, making the Belgian labor movement one of the best organized in the world.

An important dimension to unionism is the regional split that prevails in the country. The south, Wallonia, is the most heavily industrialized and least Catholic area, and it is not surprising to find the Socialist FGTB most firmly entrenched there. The Catholic CSC has its main strength—85 per cent of total membership —in Flanders, where industry and trade unionism are younger. Flanders is presently the more rapidly developing area, and this fact, plus the active support of the Church, makes the CSC somewhat more dynamic than its older, staid rival. However, a new element, composed of wartime resistance leaders, is coming to the fore in the FGTB, and they may be able to renew this union's energies.

The Belgian concept of union membership is similar to that of the United States: to remain in good standing, a worker must pay his dues regularly. Dues are about 20 francs (40 cents) a week, and because there have been few strikes since the war, the unions have become quite wealthy. Far from requiring outside subsidy, the Belgian trade unions are able to give financial assistance to political parties.

The degree of organization is not quite so high in Holland as in Belgium—only about one-half of the eligible Dutch workers belong to unions—but by any other standard, Dutch unionism is very firmly established. The Netherlands Federation of Trade Unions (NVV), which is the traditional Socialist union of the country, has about 500,000 members. The Catholic Workers' Movement (KAB) has grown rapidly since the war to reach its present level of 410,000. A third federation, distinctive to Holland, is the Protestant Labor Federation (CNV), with 225,000 members. The CNV, like the KAB, is a denominational movement, based in this case upon evangelical Calvinism. There are two Communist splinter groups, but they have been of no consequence since about 1950.

During the war, a joint council provided close liaison among the three major federations. The Socialists endeavored to bring about organizational unity in 1945, but this effort foundered on the rock of religious suspicion of socialism. All that survived was a loose Council of National Trade Union Centers to coördinate activities both nationally and locally. Even this degree of coöperation came to an abrupt end in 1954 when the Catholic Church published an episcopal mandate forbidding its members to join the NVV. In 1958, a form of regular consultation was restored, largely on the initiative of the Catholics. However, there is still some bitterness among NVV leaders, who complain that their movement is the only non-Communist movement in the world thus singled out by the Church, and that a faithful Catholic can join the Dutch Socialist party without running the risk of excommunication but not a labor union which is formally nonsectarian. Efforts to convince the Dutch Catholic hierarchy to relax its position have thus far proved unavailing.

Dutch union members pay their dues of about 1.20 guilder (30 cents) a week regularly, and all the unions are financially well established.

In Austria, as already indicated, there is a single labor federation, the Austrian Federation of Trade Unions (Oe GB), with 1.5 million members, about two-thirds of the nation's gainfully employed persons. But within the federation, which was reconstituted in 1945 after a decade of repression under fascism, there are three "fractions," which in reality are quasi-independent organizations. The Socialist fraction has about two-thirds of the total membership, the Catholic fraction 15 per cent, the Communist fraction 10 per cent, with the rest undecided. Fraction organization runs vertically throughout the entire union structure, from the local union to the Federation. At the top, there are three national party fraction confederations, each with its own newspapers, delegate bodies, and other appurtenances of self-government. To emphasize independence still further, each of the fractions has a different international affiliation, the Socialists with the International Confederation of Free Trade Unions (ICFTU), the Catholics with the Catholic trade union international, and the Communists (informally) with the World Federation of Trade Unions (WFTU).

The cause of this curious state of affairs goes back to the interwar period, when socialists and Catholics were engaged in bitter conflict which ended in civil war. When Austria regained her independence, there was universal agreement that the country could not afford a repetition of the earlier pattern of dissension. A unified labor federation was the result, but the fractions were a necessary concession to the minority groups which might otherwise have been swamped by the numerically dominant Socialists.

UNION STRUCTURE

The Belgian, Dutch, and Austrian labor movements are solidly constructed at the local level. There is no counterpart of the Italian grievance committee system to gnaw at the vitals of the movements and to limit contact between union and membership. However, local structure is somewhat different from that in the United States, and in some ways less conducive to membership participation in union affairs.

The local union in Belgium generally covers a city or other geographical area, rather than an individual plant, except in very large establishments. At the plant level, the instrument of union policy is the shop stewards' committee (*délégation syndicale*), the status of which is formalized by collective agreement. Committee members are either elected on the basis of slates proposed by the two labor movements, or simply designated by the unions in proportion to membership strength within the particular enterprise. Joint labor-management audit bodies supervise the selection of committee members, and in the unusual case of disagreement, may be called upon to determine how many committee members each union is entitled to have.

To become a shop steward, one must first be an active and loyal union man. But loyalty to one's own organization does not imply, as it too often does in Italy, antagonism to competitors, to the detriment of all constituents. In fact, a remarkable degree of coöperation between the Socialist FGTB and the Catholic CSC prevails at this level. The stewards usually share an office and often collect dues jointly. The chairmanship of the stewards' committee generally goes to the union with the preponderant membership in the plant.

The shop stewards' committee is a relatively new institution in Belgium. It was not until 1945 that employers conceded the right of negotiation at the shop level, although national bargaining was practiced much earlier. The committee is now the initial grievance-processing instance, and has the right to take up with employers all questions relating to local application of the customary national agreements. Although most stewards spend only a small part of their time on union business, in plants of more than 700 workers the chief shop steward is likely to be a full-time union officer. As a rule, he will also be a member of the local union executive committee. Belgian shop stewards are more like their American than their British namesakes: they are closely tied into the union and do not enjoy very much discretion in regard to policy.

Paralleling the shop stewards' committee are two other local bodies, the enterprise council and the committee on safety and health. The members of both are elected from lists presented by the rival unions, as with the shop stewards. The enterprise council is a consultative rather than a bargaining body, and exercises little real authority. The safety and health committees are concerned exclusively with the administration of relevant laws and agreements.

General membership meetings at the local level are held neither regularly nor frequently. Occasionally, the stewards will assemble all the workers in a plant, with the consent of the employer, to discuss a new agreement or some other issue of importance. In some industries this is general practice in the case of proposed agreements, but the meetings are usually conducted jointly by the two unions involved, rather than by each union separately.

Local meetings proper are ordinarily attended only by a small core of union activists, some of them shop stewards, who are willing to devote their free time to the conduct of union affairs. Motivated by a strong belief either in socialism or in Catholic social idealism, they provide a salutary check upon bureaucratic tendencies among permanent officials.

The local unions affiliated with a particular national union—for example, the coal mining union—are usually joined together in a regional body, and in this way constitute part of inter-industrial regional federations. For example, the CSC has such a federation in the Borinage, one of Belgium's main coal mining areas. It is run by a committee consisting of eight miners, three railroad workers, a metal worker, a civil servant, and a white collar worker, reflecting the industrial composition of CSC membership in the region. A national CSC officer is usually present to give advice at the monthly meetings of the committee, and to help prepare for the regional general assemblies, which are held three times a year. The committee often spends time reviewing the cases of individuals who are delinquent in their dues or who run into other difficulties with their unions. In 1959, the CSC had thirty-three such regional bodies in the whole country, the FGTB, twenty-six.

Belgian national unions follow industrial lines rather strictly. The FGTB has fourteen national unions affiliated with it, the CSC, seventeen. The latter organization is somewhat more centralized; for example, it maintains a central strike fund, whereas in the FGTB such funds are maintained by the national unions.

The Dutch unions are less firmly grounded locally than the Belgian. No counterpart of the Belgian shop stewards' committee exists. There is only the enterprise council, advisory in character, and usually chaired by the president of the company. The lowest union body is the local union for the city or the region, and here grievances are normally considered in the first instance. Since there are three major labor federations, every company is confronted with three separate grievance agencies, each representing its members only. The potentially disastrous competition that might result from this arrangement is averted by the fact that the unions do not attempt to outbid one another. There is a gentlemen's agreement among them to charge the same dues, and conditions of employment are the same for all workers, regardless of union membership. It is simply accepted that a worker will choose his union on the basis of politics and religion as well as economic service rendered.

Local unions try to keep contact with their members through general membership meetings, but as is everywhere the case only a minority attend meetings, and it is through these activists that the union-member link is maintained. The local union is not a very vigorous body, and in practice it is the executive board of the national union that wields the real power. Holland's peculiar system of wage determination, which will be described, has much to do with the top-heavy character of Dutch unionism.

The Socialist NVV has twenty national union affiliates, half a dozen of them being small craft unions. The Catholic federation has twenty-three national unions, and the Protestant federation about the same number. Since the war, the federations have gained authority because of the requirements of collective bargaining, but most union funds are still held by the national unions.

As long as this is true, the national unions cannot become sub-servient to the federations.

Austrian local unions, too, are organized on a city-wide rather than plant basis, each local having within it caucuses representing the three fractions. The only plant unit is the works council, which by statute is an extra-union body, elected by all those employed in the plant, from lists of candidates proposed by the three frac-tions, plus a "no-party" list. A kind of proportional representation prevails, and works council elections provide a good index of the relative strength of the fractions.

The Austrian works council is a cross between the Belgian shop stewards' and enterprise committees. It handles grievances, on the one hand, but also consults with management on general enterprise problems. In practice it has even impinged upon trade union bargaining functions, much to the displeasure of the unions. Gulick cites a prominent union official as sharing "the common union attitude that the works councils were granted too large a measure of autonomy in 1947, that they have trespassed into areas of dubious legality, and that they should be brought to the realization that they are most useful to the workers' move-ments and to society when they act as representatives of the union."[2] There is a strong feeling in union circles that too many works councils have become so concerned with the problems of their own plants that they tend to forget that more general in-terests may be involved.[3]

Much more competition prevails among the Austrian fractions than among the Belgian and Dutch federations. The Austrian Catholic fraction has a weaker hold on its members than is true of the Catholic labor federations in the other countries. Rivalry is often keen at the workshop level in Austria: one successful

---

[2] Gulick, *op. cit.*, p. 41.

[3] However, another Austrian labor official commented as follows on this statement: "Friction certainly arises on occasion between works' councils and union officials. Although a certain amount of 'Shop-Egoism' does exist, we feel that the attitude of the union official whom Professor Gulick quotes does not fairly represent the whole picture. In view of the moderate and 'responsible' wage policy of our union leadership who (like other continental unions, and unlike the Ameri-can unions) have to concern themselves with the employment effects of unfavorable export trends, the works' councils do in fact play an important role in extracting higher real wages for their workers in the more productive and prosperous firms. The differences between the wage rates fixed in the national collective agreements and the actual earnings in many firms are quite substantial. In this respect there mostly exist tacit understanding and cooperation between unions and the works' councils." Letter to the author, March 25, 1960.

socialist works councilor built himself a national reputation with the slogan, "No Communist can shout louder than I." Perhaps it is the relatively greater strength of Austrian Communism that makes the difference.

Austrian trade unionism is highly centralized—even more so than the centralized Dutch and Swedish movements. Local and district unions are often somnolent. About 80 per cent of all dues go directly to the Federation of Labor, which returns some to the national unions. Most trade union money, including strike funds, is held by the federation. All trade union officers are paid by the federation, including the officers of national unions, although the federation does not normally designate these officers.

Although in the past fifteen years most of the important bargaining decisions were made at the top, the larger national unions have begun to assert more independence, and an evolution toward decentralization may be in progress. Recent negotiations of the metal workers' and building workers' unions for relative wage increases are straws in the wind.

But, essentially, it is the fraction system which makes the Austrian labor movement much more democratic than might otherwise be the case. It is true that the fractions have no collective bargaining powers, and that the choice of a fraction by the worker is a declaration of political allegiance rather than a choice among rival unions. Yet the existence of organized factions within the trade unions, each seeking political advantage and (except for the dominant socialists) prepared to criticize the bureaucracy, cannot but serve to augment the interest of the leadership in rank and file opinion.

UNION GOVERNMENT AND POLICY

The outstanding aspect of trade unionism in the Low Countries and in Austria is the choice offered workers among competing organizations. In the United States, a worker is normally faced with the option of belonging to the union with exclusive bargaining rights over his workplace, or of abstaining from union membership, in the absence of a union shop agreement. This was less true before the AFL–CIO merger than it is now, but even in the earlier period there was unlikely to be a continuing option. Once the National Labor Relations Board makes a determination, the majority union is assured of at least a temporary, and more usually, a permanent monopoly. Few unions are able to survive lost NLRB elections for long. In Belgium, however, in addition to the nonunion option, workers may at any time choose between two permanently established unions; in Holland, among three; and in Austria, among three "fractions."

Dual unionism has always been the cardinal sin in the American labor movement. It is argued, both within the movement and by outside supporters, that the solidarity of American workers is so fragile, and employer opposition so strong, that any fragmentation will prove disastrous to the bargaining power of labor. The rise of the CIO dented the traditional concept of exclusive jurisdiction, but one of the principal aims of the merged labor movement has been to eliminate rivalry through no-raiding agreements. Although rivalry still exists in fact, it is everywhere condemned as inimical to the interests of the working man.

What is difficult for Americans to understand, therefore, is that union rivalry is accepted today in Belgium and Holland (and in Austria, fractional rivalry) as a virtue per se. This has not always been true. Before the war, religious unions were condemned as "yellow" by the Socialists, and the doctrine of unity was preached just as strongly as in the United States. But now there are few who will argue that competition among unions is any more unnatural than competition in the business world. And there is an impressive body of opinion which finds in plural unionism the best means of keeping the unions vital and democratic. Persons of this persuasion are by no means confined to intellectual bystanders, but include many highly placed union officials.

Rival unionism, in the first place, prevents the emergence of the union shop as a critical moral issue. Of course, unions might insist that workers be required to join *some* union as a condition of employment, but in fact no union is anxious to recruit for its competitors. Little pressure is exerted against the Belgian, Dutch, or Austrian worker to force him to join a union, and this cannot be attributed to the prevailingly high degree of organization. As we shall see, an equally high degree of organization in Scandinavia and in many British industries does not contribute to the exemption of the recalcitrant nonunionist.

Why, then, have workers been willing to join the unions in large numbers rather than remain free riders? It is not enough to say that there is more class consciousness than in the United States. Although this may be true as a rather vague generalization, there is the offsetting factor of deep cleavages within the working class on the basis of religion and political ideology. The ardent Communist and the devout Catholic have much to divide them, even if they are both workers.

Desire to join the Belgian unions has come from several sources. Family pressures have been particularly important in the case of the Catholic unions. Dues are often collected from the wife, who may be motivated by her religious convictions, as is her husband, that it is a moral duty to belong to a union, but who is also concerned about the strike benefit insurance provided by the unions. There have been enough strikes in postwar Belgium to make this a serious consideration. Unemployment benefits, too, may be paid either through the unions or through government offices, at the option of the insured. Many workers prefer to collect through their unions, since the payment appears less like a dole. To illustrate the importance of this consideration, the Catholic regional federation of Charleroi had 6,000 members at the beginning of 1958; a year later, after a spell of severe unemployment among coal miners, membership had risen to 9,000.

Workers are subject to a certain amount of moral suasion from their fellows. But there is neither legal disability nor moral obloquy attaching to nonmembership in a union. Few favor the union shop, and even union leaders assert that it would impair the spirit of the movement. The following extract from a recent policy statement by a Catholic union official typifies union thought on the subject:

For some time, the question of whether it is opportune to introduce some form of compulsory unionism has been much discussed in Belgium. . . . Is it necessary that a law should oblige all workers to join a union? . . . We believe that all trade unionists in Belgium are in agreement in replying negatively to this question. Among the many motives in this negative reply, the chief one is the fear that the trade union movement will lose its independence of the State, and will become an instrument of public power, similar to what has happened in countries under dictatorial control.

Specifically about the closed or union shop, he continued:

Up to now, none of these systems has been approved by the higher instances of the Christian trade union movement. For the CSC, it is important above all to conserve the independence and dynamism of trade unionism. A union which consists in part of workers who are members against their will risks becoming a bureaucracy, dedicated to immobility, and not playing its role of true champion of workers' interests.[4]

This, it must be recalled, comes from a trade union leader, and not an advocate of right-to-work legislation. Strikes to force membership are unknown, and even the check-off of union dues is regarded as an unwarranted intrusion by employers into internal union affairs (a common attitude in Europe). The Belgian national metal trades agreement contains, instead of the closed shop, the following:

The directors of enterprises belonging to the signatory employer associations undertake not to exert any pressure on their personnel to prevent them from joining a union and agree not to confer upon non-union workers any privileges not accorded union members. The signatory trade unions and the shop stewards agree to respect freedom of association, particularly in excluding from their organization techniques and methods which would not conform to the spirit of the national agreement.

A similar situation about union security provisions prevails in Holland. A closed shop exists in printing, where it has been enforced for decades, but elsewhere there is no form of compulsory membership, in spite of the fact that there are substantial numbers of unorganized workers. The Socialist NVV has an average membership turnover of 25,000 a year (of a total membership of half a million) because of job changing, emigration, and dropouts, so that recruitment of new members is a continuing problem if the ranks are not to be depleted. The Dutch unions also try to attract workers by the social services they render, although they do not pay out unemployment benefits, as in Belgium.

Austria has had a somewhat different experience with compulsory unionism, owing to the fact that there is a single labor federation even though it is divided into fractions. In many industries there is a *de facto* union shop, and since most workers who have refused to join unions are former Nazis, no one is much concerned about their right to abstain. Several years ago, in

---

[4] *Expériences*, 1958, No. 2, 131–132. In all fairness, it should be added that there are some within the labor movement who are beginning to use the "free rider" argument as the basis for advocating more pressure against non-union workers. However, the official union position is that represented by the quotation in the text.

Vienna, a few men who had once held Fascist party membership attempted to form a breakaway union and, when they were discharged from employment, entered a lawsuit against the union representatives. The issue was laid to rest when the Socialist president of the republic intervened and blocked the suit under his presidential authority. In Austria, as in Scandinavia, the power of the union is so pervasive that membership is simply taken for granted.

The second aspect of rival unionism to be considered is its effect upon the government of trade unions. There is a consensus, in the countries under discussion, that pluralism promotes "union democracy" in some sense. Given a high level of organization and security against external aggression, the existence of rival federations is regarded as stimulating and strengthening for all. The dissatisfied union member may shift his allegiance at any time with a minimum of trouble. The union must be constantly on the alert, and, as one Dutch union leader put it, "competition is as good for a union as it is for a business concern." Of the many people interviewed in Belgium and Holland, not one maintained that labor unity would be better than rivalry, given the political and religious differences that divide workers. In Austria, Socialists and Catholics would not regret seeing the Communist fraction disappear, but neither of the two main fractions desires or expects the demise of the other.

When one leaves the plane of abstraction and descends to the realities of union government, however, the democratizing effects of rival unionism are not always apparent. The monotonous tale of worker apathy toward the unions is repeated once again. Union meetings, if held at all, are poorly attended. There is little turnover of officials, and opposition in elections is a rare phenomenon. There has been a consistent trend since the war toward greater centralization in the formulation and execution of collective bargaining decisions. Permanent internal factionalism has disappeared except in Austria, although it is true that the top leadership of the Belgian FGTB is split at present on policy toward the reform of the nation's economic structure as well as on the question of the relationship of union to political party.

The fraction system of Austria has some interesting consequences for union government. The fractions do provide a forum for full and open discussion within the organization of the fraction itself. By all accounts, fraction meetings are run democratically, and an effort is made to sound out all shades of member opinion. Another aspect is that the Catholic and Communist minorities, which would be swamped by the Socialists in the normal one-party kind of union government, are given a proportional share of governmental posts and are represented at every level of union decision-making.

On the other hand, the fractions themselves, once they have come to a decision, expect every member loyally to support the majority view. Dissidence is not tolerated at this level. The system also tends to deprive formal union government of much of its operational significance. Congresses of national unions and of the federation of labor itself are to a large extent cut-and-dried affairs in which all decisions have been made beforehand by the fractions. There is agreement on the relative strength of the three groups and on the lists of candidates for office. Competition for union office is impossible, since the Socialist majority would win all the elections and drive the minorities out. All decisions must be reached by negotiation among the fraction leaders. In essence, it differs little from the rival unionism of Belgium and Holland, as far as individual members are concerned.

It should be pointed out that this peculiar Austrian system reflects the political arrangements by which the country has been governed since the war. The Socialist party and People's party, between them, control all but a handful of parliamentary representatives, and the government is a coalition of the two. Cabinet posts and many governmental offices are in effect jointly directed by representatives of the two parties: if the minister is a Socialist, the vice-minister is bound to be a People's party man, and vice versa. Once decisions are made by the cabinet, that is the end of the matter. Parliament has been reduced to a ratifying mechanism, without the power in fact to alter policies agreed upon by the leadership of the two parties.

Yet having made these observations, I must put many things on the positive side of the ledger. All the outward forms of union democracy are observed meticulously in the three countries. Conventions are held on schedule, and when statutes require, policy decisions are submitted to membership referenda. There is no cult of the individual leader, with the executive board exercising the real authority. Corruption is not only unknown, but unthinkable. Above all, one senses a real spirit of democracy and equality in the conduct of union affairs.

One is forced to the conclusion that active membership participation is not an invariable index of democracy—Communist activity should disprove any such simple relationship. Much more important is the fact that in many nations of Western Europe, including Belgium, Holland, and Austria, unionism is still an ideal. The union leader is still a crusader, perhaps no longer for a socialist society, or for some utopia, but for the economic and social betterment of what is in his view still an underprivileged class of people.

This fact is clearly reflected in the scale of living of union officials. The unions in these countries are wealthy, and could easily afford large salaries, but this would be regarded as ethically wrong. The top officers of the Belgian Catholic unions earn between $160 and $200 a month—the income of a white collar employee in industry. Some members of the union's research staff are better paid. The Socialist federation pays somewhat higher salaries, and permits its officials to sit in parliament, an arrangement which the Catholics forbid. But no trade union official approaches the earning level of even a moderately prosperous small businessman. Dutch union officials average about $3,000 a year—twice the earnings of a manual worker. Some of the highest union leaders in Austria do fairly well, because of the prevalent system of dual job holding—many of them sit in parliament or serve as members of government boards.

It is often asserted in the United States that high union salaries are essential to the maintenance of a steady flow of good leadership material. Trade unions, in this view, are actively competing with business for the best brains among the younger workers, and low union salaries would mean inferior union officers. However, in spite of the increase in social mobility that has characterized European society since the war, there does not seem to have been any dearth of willing and able candidates for union office. The Catholic unions have recruited largely through Catholic action groups. In Belgium, for example, most union leaders come out of the Christian Young Workers. The Socialist NVV, in Holland, tackled the problem as early as 1930 by setting up a leadership school which graduates about thirty persons each year. Under this scheme, the trainee spends one month at the school each year for four years, working at a factory or office job for the rest of the year. Talented young workers are urged to attend the school, which has turned out many of the present leaders of the union. It may also be noted that these unions do not make a fetish of the necessity for working class leadership; the present vice-chairman of the NVV, who is expected to attain the chairmanship, holds a degree in economics, having once served as research director of the federation.

If active membership participation is not an absolute requirement for democratic government, an informed membership may be a partial substitute, particularly if there are institutional means of sounding out opinion on critical issues. This at least is the theory on which these labor movements operate. Perhaps the best illustration is to describe the postwar collective bargaining system in Holland, which could not operate without a large measure of knowledge and consent by the individual worker.

Dutch wages have been set by national bargaining since 1945. A Board of Conciliators, first established in 1937, was endowed after the war with authority to pass judgment on all collective agreements, to fix wages and other terms of employment in the absence of agreements, and to establish general principles for the conduct of bargaining. Members of the board are not civil servants, but rather men from all walks of life, appointed by the government to represent various shades of political and economic opinion.

A so-called Foundation of Labor was set up to advise the board on policy. The foundation is bipartite, consisting of representatives of the various labor groups and employer associations. (Like the unions, Dutch employer associations are divided along religious lines, although the nonsectarian body—the Central Federation of Employers—represents 75 per cent of all employers). The labor-management wage committee of the foundation meets weekly to consider proposals made by unions and employers, and makes recommendations to the Board of Conciliators not only on national policy but on the details of wage level and structure in separate industries and plants. A national system of job evaluation has been adopted to lighten the load of determining relative wages. Nevertheless, the work load has been enormous: between 1945 and 1955, the foundation made more than 2,000 reports to the Board of Conciliators and held 5,000 meetings.

The system was changed somewhat in 1950 with the establishment of the Social Economic Council, consisting of forty-five members—fifteen each from government, labor, and management. Of the fifteen union representatives, seven are from the NVV, five from the Catholic federation, and three from the Protestant federation. This body has replaced the Foundation of Labor, which has continued as an informal forum in which issues can be discussed without government participation. The council formulates general policy on wages, leaving administration to the Board of Conciliators. But its jurisdiction is broader than wage policy; it acts in an advisory capacity on all questions of social and economic policy. For example, recently it was asked by the government for an opinion on the system of subsidies for milk and rent. The government is not obliged to follow council recommendations, but it usually does.

Union leaders are thus constantly involved in negotiations at the national level, and the consequences of economic policy are clear to them. But this is not true of the worker in the shop, and the problem is to make clear to him the rationale of the decisions adopted by the leadership.

This is a remarkable system of bargaining, but it has worked. Real wages have not risen rapidly, and indeed they were explicitly reduced in 1951 because of the impact of the Korean war upon the Dutch economy. Yet the Dutch record of industrial peace is as good as that of any nation in which workers enjoy the right to strike. Wage inflation has been modest, if present at all. The structure of wages is more rational than it was before the war, owing in no small measure to the acceptance of job evaluation on a national scale. The attitude of the unions toward productivity is much more favorable than at any time in the past; not only do they support management efforts to raise productivity, but they more or less accept productivity as a basic index in the regulation of wages.

Many factors have contributed to the smooth operation of the system. Until the end of the nineteenth century, Holland was primarily an agricultural and commercial nation, with industry lagging behind that of Belgium and Germany. Industrialization came late, and the labor force was not subjected to the worst excesses of early industrialization. Class antagonisms were consequently less acute than in other European nations. Religion has played a more important role in Holland's public life than in many other countries. Calvinism, with its emphasis upon obedience to God and to one's superior, was an important force in tempering the spirit of rebellion among workers. Income differences have been relatively small, and living standards relatively good. The

German occupation and the Allied invasion inflicted tremendous capital losses upon Holland, and coöperation of all groups was essential for national survival. The initial strain on the economy continued for a decade under the impact of the loss of Indonesia, the Korean war, and a disastrous flood in the winter of 1953. The unions—especially the Socialist NVV—are aware of the fact that a full employment policy requires a brake on the wage level. They have accepted the responsibility for applying the brake, with the proviso that the government must share in this responsibility and apply it to less well-disciplined groups. The unions are cognizant of the fact that 50 per cent of the national income of the country derives from exports. They have been convinced by economists, under the leadership of Professor Jan Tinbergen, that the economic health of the country makes wage restraint imperative in order to maintain a favorable trade balance.

Nonetheless, the trade unions were faced with a problem of no small dimensions in conveying to their members the urgency of wage restraint when wage determination had become almost a legislative function, far removed not only from local initiative but even from the national union level. The feeling grew that unions had become a kind of governmental administrative agency, and had to be counteracted lest the wage system fall under the pressure of wholesale evasion. The unions resorted to a massive educational campaign designed to justify their policies. Union publications hammered away at the nation's economic problems; leaders toured the country for discussions with groups of workers. The issue of local union atrophy was often raised in these meetings, according to some of the participants, and one of the most persuasive replies was, "Would you prefer the prewar system, with its market wage determination and heavy unemployment?" The center has had strong cards to play, for economic affairs have been well handled in Holland since the war.

There is a growing realization, however, that the system has its costs—one of the main ones being a greater distance between leadership and members. The Catholic federation is experimenting with small group discussions to bridge this gap, in the belief that the day of the mass meeting is over. The more traditional means of women's auxiliaries, vacation resorts, travel tours, and the like cannot compensate for the decline of local union function.

Symptomatic of the uneasiness with which union leadership

regards this problem is a recent split over wage policy between the Socialist NVV on the one hand and the Catholic and Protestant unions on the other. The latter have come out for less government intervention in wage fixing. They do not want complete abolition of government control, but rather limitation of its role to the determination of general policy, leaving it to the unions and employers to work out the details for themselves. The NVV, supported by the employers, oppose any relaxation of government control lest the result be inflation and the widening of wage differentials, which the Socialists oppose on ethical grounds. When one examines the opposing points of view more closely, they do not seem to be very far apart. The secretary of one of the non-Socialist federations admitted:

We have been telling our people for a long time that there is a fundamental difference between the socialists and ourselves. But they say, "You are following the same policies. What is the difference?" We want to show them that there is a difference, that we stand for more freedom from government control than the socialists.

The NVV, on its side, would also like a freer policy, but after selling the benefits of control to the members for so many years they find it difficult to turn about and preach the wisdom of market determination. The dilemma of Dutch union leadership, of whatever persuasion, is that it is convinced that a central wage policy is in the best interest of the workers and the country but it is fearful that in the long run this policy will contribute to an erosion of union strength at the grass roots level.

Late in 1959, the government instituted a "new" wage policy, linking wages to productivity industry by industry. The aim of the policy was threefold: somewhat greater differentials among industries; constant labor costs, thus destroying the validity of employer demands for price increases based upon higher wages; a constant share for wages in the national income.

The new policy, it is also claimed, will shift wage responsibility toward the individual unions. However, this has yet to be proved, because bargaining procedure remains essentially unchanged.

The Austrian trade unions have been equally responsible in their wage policy, but this was inevitable because of their tremendous power. If each national union were permitted to follow its own sectional interests, chaos would be the swift and certain outcome. Strikes cannot be lost if they have official union sanction. What has happened is that the major collective bargaining decisions are made by a few trade union leaders and politicians (all the central union figures are also politicians) at the cabinet level. There is a great deal of grumbling about this system but, to judge by the almost complete absence of illegal strikes and any other form of demonstration, also complete acquiescence in it. The Austrian worker has had his fill of revolution and war, and is satisfied to entrust decision-making to his leaders as long as his material standards keep advancing.

Rival unionism is evidently no universal panacea for membership apathy. However, it does have certain advantages in augmenting freedom of choice. But the question may properly be raised, is this at the expense of union effectiveness, and if so, how is one to balance the collective cost against the individual gain?

Fortunately, it is not necessary to confront the two desiderata, for there is no evidence that single unions could have accomplished any more for their members than was achieved under conditions of rival unionism. On the contrary, it may be that competition kept the unions more alert than they might otherwise-have been. In Belgium, for example, the Catholic union movement was the first to initiate a drive for shorter working hours when a Socialist government was in power. The Socialist FGTB had to follow along, even though it meant disagreement with the government party with which it was allied. Now that there is a Catholic government, the FGTB is seeking to take the initiative in economic reform, and the Catholic unions cannot afford to be left behind. Whipsawing may have disadvantages for economic stability, but it does keep the unions alive. The Protestant unions in Holland, which are rather conservative in their outlook, are propelled in large measure by their competitors.[5]

---

[5] The following quotation from a statement by the intellectual leader of Dutch Protestant trade unionism illustrates the handicaps under which this movement is operating in its appeals for labor support: "It is not . . . ever shorter working hours for which the Christian social movement is striving. Labor is essential to man. It is in developing the possibilities hidden in creation that he fulfills his godly vocation. The too great a shortening of working hours results in decadence, and promotes indulgence in lower pleasures. . . . That's why the 48-hour week is no dogma. We can safely say that for the normal industrial relations in Western Europe it marks about the right line between the times for working and resting. In countries that suffered badly from the late war and which in consequence have to take full recourse to the original source of making capital, viz., labor, it may be a duty to accept longer hours, the shift-system and such, exactly because labor is man's vocation." W. F. de Gaay Fortman, *Aims and Purposes of Christian Trade-Unionism*, (Utrecht: 1958) pp. 5–6.

But it is not necessarily true that a system of labor market organization which has yielded satisfactory results in Belgium, Holland, and Austria will prove of equal merit elsewhere. Rather, it seems that certain conditions must first be met and that, in their absence, the encouragement of rival unionism might be a hazardous undertaking.

First and most important, the labor movement as a whole must be immune to crippling attacks by employers, and collective bargaining must gain full acceptance. We need only cite France and Italy as examples of what rival unionism may produce in the absence of union security.

Sharp divisions among workers as to political beliefs, religion, and culture provide a logical setting for union pluralism. Dutch society is sometimes referred to as being organized on the "pillar" system, in which all social institutions are segregated vertically along religious lines. In such circumstances, unified trade unionism is fraught with tremendous difficulties and, even if it can be achieved, can cause great internal tensions. Rival unionism seems to be a preferable way of working out an accommodation among the different points of view.

A general consensus on economic means and goals is essential to the accomplishment of interunion accommodation. This is unlikely, for example, where a strong Communist movement exists, and it was not true in prewar Belgium, Holland, and Austria. But wartime coöperation, the requirements of reconstruction, and a surprising degree of agreement on economic theory and policy have contributed toward the necessary consensus. Whether this will continue, now that economic necessities have become less urgent, remains to be seen.

UNIONS AND POLITICS

As already noted, the traditional unionism of Belgium, Holland, and Austria was Socialist-oriented. In Belgium and Holland an attenuated form of social democratic doctrine held sway, the union movements there having been far to the right in the spectrum of European labor ideology. Austrian Socialism was quite a different matter, for this was one of the more radical non-Communist movements, and its record of resistance to fascism demonstrated that it was militant in deed as well as in word.

The alienation of Belgian and Dutch trade unionism from its

socialist origins has proceeded apace since the war. Both the Belgian FGTB and the Dutch NVV are moving away from alliance with the Socialist parties of their countries. This reflects in part a reassessment of the possibilities of achieving economic gains through the instrumentality of the parties. It is no accident that where trade union ties with the Socialists are still strong, as in Austria, the Socialist party has a potentiality for the attainment of governmental power. The Austrian Socialist party has polled about 45 per cent of the total votes cast in recent parliamentary elections, whereas the comparable figures for Belgium and Holland are 36 per cent and 28 per cent respectively. There is no great attraction in tying one's fortunes to a permanent minority movement.

In 1945, the Belgian Socialist party switched from collective affiliation of trade union members to a pattern of individual membership quite apart from the unions. This was not entirely a voluntary renunciation, for during the war, a left-wing syndicalist faction grew up in the underground labor movement, opposed to close ties with any political party. André Renard, the leader of this tendency, became president of the Metal Workers' Union, an organization which to this day does not permit its officers to sit in Parliament, a departure from Belgian custom. Renard is now assistant general secretary of the Socialist FGTB, and heads the powerful faction which favors complete separation of trade union and political party. The only remaining mechanism of coöperation is Common Action, which was established in 1949 to coördinate the activities of the Socialist party, the FGTB, and the coöperative movement. The committee has not worked well, to the sorrow of the Socialist party leaders.

There are still close personal ties between the trade union and political movements. About half the FGTB executives are Socialist members of Parliament, and most Socialist party members are also in the FGTB. Whether the distance will widen or narrow depends upon the outcome of factional struggles within each organization. The left-wing FGTB unions, supported by a minority within the party, are sharply critical of the party's economic policy from 1954 to 1958, when it was in a government coalition in partnership with the Liberal party. The critics charge that the Socialists paid the heavy price for Liberal support of failing to tackle the basic problem of structural unemployment. Now out

38

of office, the Socialist party has moved to the left, and is advocating nationalization of the coal, gas, and electric power industries as well as government control of banks and financial houses. A Catholic-Socialist coalition would be necessary to effect these reforms, and some of the trade unionists are prepared to make the necessary ideological concessions. Whether the Socialists will go along remains to be seen; in any event, Catholic misgivings make such a coalition unlikely for the time being.

The Belgian CSC is one of a number of Catholic action organizations that blanket the country. One of the six members of its executive committee is a priest appointed by the Church authorities, although he does not participate in economic policy-making. The relationship of CSC to the Christian Social party, which is once again the leader in a coalition government, is complicated by the fact that the party represents not only workers, but a complete cross section of economic interest groups. Businessmen, professionals, and farmers are as important as workers in party councils.

In order to avoid responsibility for the acts of the Christian Social party, the CSC forbids its full time officials to sit in Parliament or even to serve as mayors and aldermen in the larger cities. Coöperation between the two movements depends largely on the character of party leadership at any particular time. The present Catholic prime minister, Gaston Eyskens, is personally close to the social and economic viewpoint of the CSC, but his government depends for its parliamentary majority upon the business-oriented Liberal party. There are those in both the FGTB and the CSC who feel that a new grouping of labor-oriented Socialist and Catholic unionists in the political arena would be desirable, but a whole host of vested interests blocks any development of this character.

It might be argued from this that rival unionism in Belgium weakens the power of labor by blunting its political impact through diffusion into political organizations which are kept apart by noneconomic ideological considerations. But ideology is as important to the workers as to any other social group, and a unified trade union movement could be kept together only by observing the strictest kind of political and religious neutrality. Whether this would further the economic well-being of workers is at least questionable. Perhaps having a foot in each political camp is a superior arrangement, even if the footing is not always steady. At least the union movement as a whole never finds itself in opposition to the government in power.

The Dutch experience lends support to this conclusion. As in Belgium, the close organizational prewar ties between the NVV and the Labor party were severed in 1945. Now there is not even a joint committee, let alone collective affiliation of union members in the party. Article 3 of the revised NVV constitution states that "the Federation considers it to be undesirable to constitute trade unions based on denominational or ideological considerations." But there are still many personal links between the two organizations.

In contrast with Belgium, there are no serious differences of opinion on policy within the NVV or the Labor party. The Labor party was a partner in a government coalition from 1945 to 1959, and as such shared in the responsibility for stringent fiscal measures which had a particularly severe impact upon the middle class. Now that it is in the opposition, it is going to have to make a choice between the lower tax demands of this class, and trade union insistence that high taxation is essential to the enlargement of government social services. Although there is a small group within the party which would like to see a more radical program, this is not likely to emerge from the present search for a new ideology.

The Dutch Catholic trade unions are joined to the Catholic People's party by a common ideology. The Protestant labor federation is in a more difficult position, for although six of its officers are in Parliament, they are split between two Protestant parties. Again, as in Belgium, the non-Socialist parties appeal to all social groups, not just workers. The government which took office in 1959 is more employer- than worker-minded, and all the federations may be obliged to fight it on specific issues. There has been some coöperation on an extra-party level; for example, the president of each of the federations is a member of the Dutch Senate, and they have constituted themselves an unofficial labor caucus.

The fractions within the Austrian Federation of Trade Unions are as much political as economic bodies. Although the federation is formally nonpartisan by virtue of its universal character, in practice there is the closest coöperation between unions and parties. Many trade union leaders, including some from the Catholic fraction, sit in Parliament. Local party organizations

40

are often required to accept union officers as their nominees so that the unions can have adequate parliamentary representation.

The Austrian Socialist party has about 700,000 members, at least five-sixths of whom come from the ranks of the nation's more than two million employees. Funds from union dues cannot be used for political purposes, but the union fractions raise political money on a voluntary basis. As long as the Socialists are part of the coalition governing the country, the workers will be well represented in national affairs. Should the Socialists enter into opposition at some future time, the relative weakness of Catholic political action among workers would mean that labor would face a largely hostile political environment.

Belgium, Holland, and Austria constitute a prime example of the viability of rival unionism and of its beneficent effects on union democracy. The workers of these countries can choose as freely among unions as among political parties, and the unions are consequently inhibited from taking their constituents for granted. Trade union membership (except perhaps in Austria) is entirely voluntary in character, and there are not the undertones of middle-class resentment of unions that exist in many other countries.

But, as I have already stressed, we cannot generalize too readily from this experience. Rival unionism works well because, in the first place, all the unions enjoy security, and need not concern themselves with the problems arising out of employer hostility. Second, deep religious and political differences among the workers would make a unified labor movement difficult to achieve, so that a policy of "live and let live" may be the only alternative to destruction of all labor organization. Finally, common wartime experiences among labor leaders of all persuasions served to dispel historical animosities which might otherwise have persisted and made coöperation difficult.

Notwithstanding these limitations, the Belgian-Dutch-Austrian model is worth further study, for here is one of the few situations in which competition among unions has proved its worth. The widely held belief that union rivalry is necessarily detrimental to worker interests is at least called into question by the existence of one good example to the contrary.

CHAPTER III. THE STRENGTH OF UNIFIED TRADE UNIONISM: GREAT BRITAIN AND SCANDINAVIA

British and Scandinavian labor relations provide the most familiar terrain for one acquainted with the American labor scene. Strong united trade union movements and collective bargaining are well established. The collective agreement (in Scandinavia, though not always in Britain) is typically a long, formidable document, regulating many aspects of the job in addition to wages. Political action is an important supplement to collective bargaining, though the form it takes varies from one country to another.

Because of these underlying resemblances, the contrast that emerges under closer scrutiny is the more useful. We are likely to learn less from France and Italy or the Low Countries than from Britain and Scandinavia. In Britain, a common language and system of laws render the institutions that have grown up of particular interest to us.

42

There is available an extensive body of literature on recent industrial relations in these countries, making it unnecessary to describe their practices in any detail.[1] What I have attempted to do instead is to stress the specific aspects which are most relevant to our inquiry.

GREAT BRITAIN

The Trades Union Congress (TUC) stands unchallenged at the apex of the trade union world in Great Britain. About eight and a half million workers belong to one or another of its more than seven hundred affiliated unions, which vary in size from the giant general unions to craft organizations confined to single localities. The movement is, in fact, rather concentrated; about fifteen unions have 70 per cent of total TUC membership. Some 44 per cent of all gainfully employed persons are trade unionists, an impressive degree of organization.

But the power of British unionism cannot be measured simply in quantitative terms. To quote a recent study of their place in British society:

Their influence has been enhanced, in the first place, by acceptance of the 'tripartite principle' in administrative arrangements dating mainly from the war, ranging from local productivity committees up to the Joint Production Advisory Council and to informal discussions between the Trades Union Congress and cabinets, of whatever color. The unions' actual bargaining power in the labor market has been reinforced by the extension of publicly regulated negotiation through wage councils, labor boards and arbitration machinery. And they have benefited greatly from the spread of government influence in the economy. Wherever it has gone, into nationalized industries, social services, subsidized agriculture, the government has conceded trade union recognition to all its direct and indirect employees as a matter of course.[2]

Once the turmoil of war and postwar reconstruction had receded into the past, and the nation was settled down for the long

---

[1] See Allan Flanders and Hugh Clegg, *The System of Industrial Relations in Great Britain* (Oxford: Oxford University Press, 1954); B. C. Roberts, *Trade Union Government and Administration in Great Britain* (Cambridge: Harvard University Press, 1956); Walter Galenson, *Labor in Norway* (Cambridge: Harvard University Press, 1949); Walter Galenson, *The Danish System of Industrial Relations* (Cambridge: Harvard University Press, 1952). There is no recent study for Sweden. The last full length treatment is Paul H. Norgren, *The Swedish Collective Bargaining System* (Cambridge: Harvard University Press, 1941).

[2] *The Economist*, February 8, 1958.

pull, the question of how trade union power was to be employed came to the fore. There has been increasing public scrutiny of labor's methods. Adverse press comment, some judicial decisions, and rank and file restiveness have contributed to a considerable amount of soul-searching within the labor movement. One of the subjects which has come in for closest examination is that of individual member rights.

LOCAL ORGANIZATION AND THE SHOP STEWARDS

The lowest formal structural unit in most British national unions is the branch. In some unions, such as the Mineworkers, branch jurisdiction is coterminous with the workplace. Usually the branch takes in a specified geographical area, including a number of separate shops. Branches have been growing larger, partly because of ease of administration.

Along with the growth of branch size has also grown an apathetic attitude of members toward union affairs. B. C. Roberts reports that average membership attendance at branch meetings in the larger unions falls in a range of three to fifteen present, with a concentration usually between four and seven.[3] The secretary of a branch of the Printers, Bookbinders and Paper Workers Union in a medium-sized city told me that the quarterly meetings of his organization were attended almost exclusively by minor union officials, and that a special meeting called in 1959 to discuss national contract demands (a strike, the first since 1926, eventually resulted) was attended by exactly sixty-eight persons of a branch membership of fifteen hundred. Clegg, in his study of the National Union of General and Municipal Workers, the second largest union in Britain, found that a regular attendance of one hundred in a branch of three thousand was regarded as a good performance.[4] One is told approximately the same story everywhere.

Branch meetings are conducted in an honest and democratic fashion, by all accounts. Union statutes generally provide for regular meetings, and stipulate that they must begin and end at certain times, to prevent rump sessions inconvenient to members. There is no evidence of suppression of minority views, and in fact, Communists have been able to take advantage of low attendance

---

[3] B. C. Roberts, *op. cit.*, p. 95.
[4] Hugh Clegg, *General Union* (Oxford: Oxford University Press, 1954), p. 40.

to gain influence in branch affairs far out of proportion to their numbers.

The term of office of branch secretaries varies. In some unions, election is for life; in others, reëlection is required periodically. It makes little difference, however, because once a man is elected he can usually retain the position as long as he wants it. Only on the occasion of a branch secretary's retirement is there likely to be any contest for the office. One reason is that the job is not a particularly attractive one; the typical branch secretary usually earns little more than the branch's members.[5] In the printing trades branch referred to earlier, the secretary was being paid £13 a week, whereas he had previously been earning £16 as a bookbinder. Expense accounts and outside sources of income are generally not available to branch secretaries. To most of them, union office is not a business but a calling. Corruption is a rare phenomenon. The parade of recalcitrant local union officers that appeared before the McClellan Committee was regarded with amazement and bewilderment by the British trade union world.

At an earlier period in British labor history, branch meetings were better attended and membership participation was more active. What accounts for the atrophy of the branch? One factor is undoubtedly the trend toward national wage bargaining. Although branch meetings are called to discuss wage proposals, the members feel—quite rightly—that there is little they can do to influence the negotiations. Then too, the growth of branch size and the failure of most unions to develop an adequate professional leadership corps at the local level have tended to divorce the branch from workshop problems. The branch has been losing its major function and becoming a kind of dues collector for the national union. No wonder the British worker prefers to stay home with his television set rather than go to a drafty union hall where nothing of interest is happening.

There are important workshop problems to be handled, however, and the failure of the branch to tackle them adequately has given rise to a significant development in union structure—the proliferation of shop stewards. This is by no means a new phenomenon, for during the First World War there was a concerted shop stewards' movement which caused much trouble for the unions. The present upsurge seems to be more widespread, however, and

---

[5] These remarks apply to the few hundred out of the 40,000 branch secretaries who have full time positions. The rest of them do branch work in their spare time.

bids fair to persist. It is one of the major objects of concern to British unionism at the present time.

The position of the shop steward varies greatly from industry to industry, and from union to union. In some instances he is "unofficial" in that neither union rules nor collective agreement makes any provision for him. The General and Municipal Workers, for example, did not give any recognition to shop stewards until 1951, when a limited status was accorded. At the other extreme is the Amalgamated Engineering Union, which has integrated the shop steward into its structure by giving him representation on dictrict executive committees, alongside the branches, and outside of branch control. The giant Transport and General Workers Union follows an intermediate procedure. Its 25,000 shop stewards are recognized as union agents, but are closely controlled by the branches.

The resurgence of the shop steward movement during the Second World War coincided with the development of joint production committees to maximize output for the war effort. The labor representatives for these committees had to be drawn from the shop. When the committees were terminated at the end of the war, it was natural for the labor committeemen to continue on as informal grievancemen. Their opportunity arose because of the poverty of the branches; there are now only 3,000 full time paid officials to serve the 40,000 branches and eight and a half million members of the unions affiliated with the TUC. Branch and district officials found themselves unable to handle the growing membership of their organizations, and they were forced, often reluctantly, to permit stewards to assume traditional branch functions.

It is difficult to generalize about the authority of the shop steward in contemporary Britain. Where there is more than one union in an enterprise, which is common because of the absence of the exclusive-jurisdiction concept, the shop steward provides a means of interunion cooperation. In such instances, of which engineering is typical, the shop stewards' committee may become a nearly independent body—a union within a union—negotiating on a whole range of matters including wages above the national scale. To cite an example, the Metropolitan Vickers aircraft plant in Manchester, with 20,000 workers, has some twenty different unions. There are common problems, such as redundancy and transfer, which cannot possibly be handled by twenty different branches, so that the stewards are given considerable latitude. In the basic steel industry, by way of contrast, there is usually only one union at a plant, and the shop stewards, where they exist, have only limited power.

What sort of a person is the shop steward likely to be? The following is a portrait drawn by one who knows the movement well:

The shop steward is notoriously a radical in the trade union movement —he sees the hardships under which he and his fellows work without the opportunity of appreciating the wider industrial and political problems which complicate the settlement of his grievances. He is a trade unionist and proud of it—a most essential link in modern trade union organization—but his job is mainly in industry and not in the branch. Consequently he may have common interests with other workers which transcend trade union boundaries. Joint shop stewards' committees may be formed in the works and local or national shop stewards' movements have sprung up from time to time. The first are frequently recognized by the union, the latter rarely, so that they are unofficial. In times of stress, extremists—including communists—often come to the front in such unofficial bodies; and in quiet intervals it is the extremists who keep their organization alive.[6]

The British Communist party has had its greatest success among the shop stewards. A number of practices surrounding the institution help account for this: the shop steward normally has no contract protection, so that the job may be somewhat risky, leaving the way open for the ardent radical; there is rarely any pay, except for reimbursement of out-of-pocket expenses; the manner in which stewards are elected is haphazard, usually by a show of hands, permitting an organized minority to dominate the proceedings; the ladder to higher union office does not begin with the position of shop steward in many unions, since the stewards often find themselves in conflict with the union officialdom.

The reluctance of the unions to face up to the emergence of the shop stewards has been reinforced by Communist influence among them. There is a fear that to incorporate them into the union structure, as the Amalgamated Engineering Union has, will merely open the way for Communist infiltration into the national union. But the unions are being forced to take steps in the direc-

---

[6] Clegg, *op. cit.*, p. 117.

tion of regularizing the stewards because they fill an obviously vital need in the shop.

British unions have had considerable experience in handling Communists, and at the present time there is little prospect for an expansion of Communist influence. The Transport and General Workers simply barred Communists from all union offices in 1949. The General and Municipal Workers have not gone that far, but "the Executive, relying on its 'absolute discretion' to determine standards for full-time officers, and its authority to remove such officers for any reason it 'considers good and sufficient' would not allow any open communist or sympathizer to obtain a full-time post, and would remove a convert."[7] Although this policy has inhibited the growth of Communist influence within the formal union structure, it has tended to push Communist activists into shop steward posts, the only outlet for their organizational ambitions.

Another aspect of the shop steward problem that is even more disturbing to thoughtful Britons is the appearance of a new type of steward, motivated neither by commitment to the ideal of union service nor by a left wing ideology, but rather by sheer self-interest. What this person seeks is the satisfaction of power, exemption from hard work (in larger plants, shop stewards often spend most of the time away from their jobs), and in some instances, especially where there are organized lotteries to finance local activities, the possibility of picking up some extra money. A recent article noted that "the descent from a partly politically inspired movement into a plain and powerful racket can be made in easy stages, especially when the words 'union solidarity' can be used as a holy cloak; and it is in this section of activities that a Royal Commission into trade unionism would most probably dredge up some elements of the sort of irregularity which congressional inquiries have discovered in America."[8]

British trade union purity has so long been taken for granted that this problem has never been investigated, so that the observation quoted above can be neither affirmed nor refuted by appeal to the facts. But the bland assumption that corruption is completely nonexistent[9] would seem to require at least some check-

---

[7] Clegg, *op. cit.*, p. 121.

[8] *The Economist*, "Where the Danger Lies," Vol. CLXXXVI, p. 464, February 15, 1958.

[9] See, for example, B. C. Roberts, *Unions in America* (Princeton: Princeton University Press, 1954), p. 134.

ing. No one would quarrel with the statement that the problem in Britain has altogether different dimensions than in the United States; it is a matter of possible petty theft versus grand larceny. However, British shop stewards (not union officials) often find themselves in situations which are ideal for graft—they have considerable power without responsibility.

For this as well as other reasons, British unionism is going to have to come to grips with the problem of local structure. The shop steward has come forward as a makeshift substitute for the branch, fulfilling a function which the latter has failed to perform adequately. If the shop steward is suppressed, the result is likely to be a deepening of member apathy; if he is permitted to operate unofficially, abuses will undoubtedly creep in, if they have not done so already. Integration into union structure, following the usual practice in the United States, seems to be the logical solution, although multiple unionism makes this a more difficult accomplishment. Whatever the final result, British unionism will have to make its peace with this latest manifestation of rank and file revolt.

THE UNOFFICIAL STRIKE

A closely allied problem, which has become acute in the last few years, is that of the unofficial strike. It is probably fair to say that no country in Europe suffers more from this puzzling outbreak of direct action, in contravention of all union rules and collective agreements. In the last half of 1954, such strikes affected, among others, the railway dining cars, the Sheffield buses, the Liverpool tugs, the Renault works at Acton, the Gloworm Boiler Works, the Bankside power station, and a General Electric refrigerator plant. It is scarcely necessary explicitly to add British automobile plants to the list, so common a phenomenon has the wildcat strike become in that sector. In October, 1959, the TUC appointed a committee to investigate the activities of shop stewards and their connection with unofficial strikes, thus bringing to the level of formal recognition what has long been a subject of ardent informal discussion within the labor movement.

The overt causes of unofficial strikes are many: a reduction in force, rationalization of work processes, the refusal of a worker to join a union, jurisdictional disputes, wage grievances. In many instances, the strikes are directed as much against the union as against the employer. Justifiably or not, many workers have felt that their union was not representing their interests with sufficient vigor, and it has not been difficult to convince them that direct strike action was their only redress.

The response of the unions varies with the circumstances. When an unofficial strike is led by Communists, of either orthodox or dissident varieties, an attempt may be made to break it by expelling the ringleaders from union membership and ordering the rest back to work. Greater caution is exercised when the strike leadership is non-Communist, particularly if branch officials are in sympathy with the strikers—as, for example, when the purpose of the strike is to force 100 per cent membership or to assert a jurisdictional claim. National unions cannot justify these strikes, but they may find themselves obliged to support them because of the force of membership opinion.

There are no legal ways to prevent unofficial strikes in Great Britain, which is one of the barriers to the union's control. An unofficial strike has the same immunities from legal prosecution as one sanctioned by the union. Most collective agreements do not have specified terms, and may be abrogated at any time. Generally speaking, there is no provision, as in American agreements, for final arbitration of grievances that cannot be settled by negotiation; the ultimate means of settlement is work stoppage. It has been suggested that the hand of the unions would be strengthened if only those strikes sanctioned by formal union action were exempted from criminal or civil attack, but the unions are understandably not at all happy about the prospect of opening up any breach in the immunities which they have managed to put into the law over the years.

Many unofficial strikes are called by shop stewards without consulting their fellow workers, who know about it for the first time when they are told to stop work. The proposal has been made that a ballot of those affected should be required before a strike can legally begin. The National Union of Mineworkers does require a referendum before strikes may be called; yet, in 1956, some 78 per cent of all the unofficial strikes in the country were in coal mining. It is one thing to enact a law against strikers and another to enforce it, especially when there are no union funds available for attachment. Moreover, shop stewards would not ordinarily find it hard to obtain strike majorities in the name of union solidarity, and their authority would thereby be strengthened.

The whole matter will be aired by the special TUC committee that has been established, but whether anything can be done is questionable. Perhaps the unofficial strike is a democratic necessity as a check upon trade unions which have become so respectable and responsible that they are beginning to lose touch with their members. The workers of Britain are not of a revolutionary frame of mind, and have not been so for a century, but there is still among them a strong sense of protest against the obvious social and economic inequalities that persist in Britain. If unions confine themselves to a species of administrative wage setting far removed from the individual, some vent will have to be found for release of the tensions that build up from feelings of injustice. To quote a close student of the British labor movement:

The fact that these rebellions occur indicates that local unions' leaders are not cowed, tyrannical individuals, completely ground down by the bureaucratic machinery of modern industrial relations, and it might be claimed that so far as stewards, and the ordinary members who follow their lead, are not prepared to accept any situation pressed upon them without demur, unofficial strikes are a healthy manifestation.[10]

THE NATIONAL UNION AND ITS LEADERS

British national unions are run with scrupulous care for democratic forms. The only exception appears to be a few Communist-controlled unions which have been charged with ballot box stuffing. However, there are great variations among unions in responsiveness to membership opinion. Unions can be ranked by degree of internal democracy, depending in part on the character of leadership and the institutions of union government.[11]

The principal officer of a British national union is ordinarily the general secretary, rather than the president. In most unions, he has permanent tenure until he reaches the mandatory retirement age, usually sixty-five. Some organizations require periodic

---

[10] Roberts, *Trade Union Government*, p. 461.
[11] See the remarks of Hugh Clegg in Michael Harrington and Paul Jacobs, *Labor in a Free Society* (Berkeley and Los Angeles: University of California Press, 1954), pp. 136–38.

reëlection, but since an incumbent is almost never defeated this has little effect on length of term in office.[12] There has been some discussion of whether election for a lifetime term is democratic. Proponents of the practice, who are in the majority in the British union world, argue that security of tenure promotes efficient administration and enables officials to determine policy without regard to political consequences. As long as there is an ultimate power in the executive council or the delegate conference to remove an obviously unfit officer, there does not seem to be any inherent vice in the system, particularly when it is recalled that turnover will be slight in any event. In fact, the British general secretary conforms more to the model of the civil servant than to the American-style union president. He is paid a relatively modest salary. Only five general secretaries earn more than £2,000 annually, with £2,500 ($7,000) the maximum amount paid anyone. The smaller unions pay between £1,000 and £1,500. Expense accounts, moreover, are usually under strict control. Some alienation of national leaders from rank and file is inevitable, if only because the former lead totally different ways of life. Their time is taken up by conferences, meetings with government officials, and speeches; they are completely divorced from factory work. There is also the peculiarly British practice of conferring titles on deserving union leaders, which contributes further to setting them apart. From a materialistic standpoint, however, there is none of the conspicuous consumption indulged in by many American union officers, and the idea that a British union leader could carry on a business for profit alongside his union duties would be met with incredulity.

Another contrast with the United States lies in the constitutional powers vested in the chief executive of a union.

No British trade union gives its general secretary the almost unlimited power of appointing and suspending union officers, controlling union funds, branch activities and policies and interpreting union rules, which is enjoyed, for example, by the presidents of the Railway Clerks Union, the United Mine Workers or the Amalgamated Clothing Workers in the United States.[13]

The general secretary works under the supervision of the execu-

---

[12] In a study of 128 elections involving twenty-four unions, there were only two instances in which an incumbent general secretary was defeated.

[13] Roberts, *Trade Union Government,* p. 281.

tive board, and the amount of administrative freedom he enjoys depends on his relations with the board. He may have authority to hire and fire headquarters' office staff and to act against district or local officials in emergency situations, if he reports to the board at the earliest opportunity. But normal disciplinary action against officers or rebellious branches would always be a matter for the board.

The executive boards of many British unions are composed in whole or in part of lay members, who are working at the trade and are not paid by the union except for time lost and expenses incurred in attending board meetings. The purpose of the lay executive is to keep the officers in touch with rank-and-file opinion and to curb official action which is at variance with membership sentiment. Whether practice bears out the theory is a matter of some controversy. Roberts, while recognizing the limitations of the device, favors it, and in prescribing for reform of the American labor movement, declares: "It would be a healthy development if the senior officers of unions were subject to the control of an executive committee of the rank and file."[14] One of the top officers of the TUC told me recently that he regards this as the most democratic aspect of British unionism.

There are others, however, who have some doubts about the efficacy of the lay executive in keeping a rein upon union leadership. The experience of the two largest unions in the country—the Transport and General Workers and the National Union of General and Municipal Workers—may be cited as cases in point. The founder of the former and its first general secretary, Ernest Bevin, laid great stress upon the value of the lay executive, of which he was a nonvoting ex-officio member:

By referring most matters to the Executive before taking action, Bevin did not reduce his power as a leader; he was still able to take the initiative, but whether or not he retained it depended on his ability to convince the Executive members with his arguments. . . . His method possessed two main advantages. Firstly it considerably strengthened his position as a union representative. . . . Secondly it had a profound psychological effect on the Executive members, for it was they who were determining policy even though it was under his astute guidance.[15]

---

[14] Roberts, *Unions in America*, p. 40.
[15] V. L. Allen, *Trade Union Leadership* (Cambridge: Harvard University Press, 1957), p. 86.

Bevin's successor, Arthur Deakin, had a different relationship with his executive. "To some extent he changed the character of Executive meetings; they became more concerned with receiving reports rather than with formulating lines of future action, and consequently had less to say than in Bevin's day."[16] For the first few years of Deakin's regime, the executive was a more lively body because of election to it of a group of Communists: nine of the thirty-four members. But in 1949, the convention of the national union declared Communists ineligible to hold any union office, and this bloc was eliminated. Deakin proved to be a ruthless leader, not hesitating on occasion to brand his political opponents as Communists even when this charge was not true. Under the present general secretary, Frank Cousins, the executive has continued to be a fairly quiescent body, deferring to him on policy questions.

Several factors make it possible for a lay executive to fall under the domination of a general secretary, as seems to have taken place within the Transport and General Workers. First, there is likely to be a good deal of turnover among the lay members. From 1942 to 1952, there was an average change of 50 per cent in the T and GWU executive council membership between biennial elections, owing to retirements and appointments to full-time union office. Though in one sense rapid turnover of executive membership is all to the good, in that it prevents the lay members from becoming too professionalized, short tenure keeps them from acquiring sufficient knowledge of union affairs to match the permanent general secretary. Another, more serious, consideration is the pattern of appointment to union office. Regional and district officers are appointed by the executive council in the Transport and General Workers, with the general secretary exerting considerable influence. Many lay executive members aspire to union office, and may be fearful of opposing the general secretary lest they be branded as unorthodox. In organizations like the Amalgamated Engineering Union and the Vehicle Builders which elect their district officers, there is usually more freedom of discussion within the executive.

The General and Municipal Workers have a general council of which half are paid officers and half are lay members. H. A. Clegg found that it was not always easy to distinguish between the two

---

[16] *Ibid.*, p. 250.

groups, since the lay members spent a good deal of time on union business. However, the lay members were overshadowed by the senior officers, though these, in turn, had more status vis-à-vis the general secretary because of their membership on the council. But the lay members did have one powerful weapon: they constituted a special subcommittee to handle officers' salaries, and to this extent controlled the purse strings.[17]

These unions may be compared with the Amalgamated Engineering Union, which has a full-time executive committee, with each member having divisional administrative and negotiating responsibilities. Here the executive committee is more powerful relative to the general secretary than is true in the two large general unions. The fact that the members are elected in their districts and have independent political bases contributes significantly to this result. One consequence is that the national union has relatively less authority over its regional and divisional units. Nor does a weaker central leadership necessarily imply greater rank-and-file participation. In a hotly fought election in 1959 which received national press attention, W. J. Carron was elected general secretary over R. Birch, his Communist opponent, by a vote of 57,000 to 18,000, out of 960,000 members eligible to vote.

There seems to be no simple correlation between the degree of democracy in union government and the composition of the national executive. On balance, one may fairly conclude that with all its limitations, the lay executive is a sound device for the prevention of autocracy. An officer will think twice before defying a committee which is the embodiment of the rank and file. He will rather attempt to persuade, and will compromise if sentiment runs strongly against him.

Both officers and executive committee are subject to control by delegate conferences, and in some unions by intermediate bodies. The annual conference—usually large—does not perform effectively. It is rare for the platform to be overruled on an issue of any importance, and the conference committees are generally controlled from the top. The Amalgamated Engineering Union has a smaller rank-and-file delegate council of 52 members, which has restrained the executive on many occasions. The Webbs favored this representative device as against the larger conference. Whatever weaknesses large bodies may have, however, they are

---

[17] Clegg, *op. cit.*, pp. 344–346.

far better than nothing. The Iron, Steel and Kindred Trades Association has no periodic delegate meeting, and it is regarded as one of the least democratic unions in Britain. Recently, the officers of a Welsh branch who opposed the policies of the national union were barred from holding office for life; when they were supported by other branches, similar treatment was meted out to their colleagues. Such action is rare in Britain, because the national officials would have to account to an indignant rank and file.

There is no simple answer about the value of the referendum as a democratic method. Many unions require that their members be polled in advance of a strike, but since the leadership can always get a strike majority if it wants one, this is of little importance. Some unions use the referendum in connection with new contracts, but again the officials are rarely rebuffed. For example, the printing unions, in 1959, sent out ballots in which the employer policy of "total rejection" of union demands was denounced, and the members were asked to vote Yes or No on whether they backed the stand of their officials in refusing to accept the terms offered by the employers. The only surprising thing about this vote was that 20 per cent of the members responding voted to accept.

Occasionally, the referendum may prove to be an effective policy instrument. Recently, the Communist-dominated executive of the Electrical Trades Union decided to affiliate with the British Peace Council, a Communist-front organization. Under the constitution, 10 per cent of the branches could force a referendum on any policy issue. There was a complication in that branches are forbidden to communicate with one another directly, but have to go through the national union, which could have been relied upon to block any action. To circumvent this restriction, officers of the Canterbury branch formed the Canterbury Electricians' Committee as an informal body, and circularized other branches for support of a resolution condemning the act of the executive. The required number of branches endorsed the referendum, which resulted in defeat of the leadership by a two to one margin. For their pains, however, the Canterbury branch officers were deposed and barred from union office for from two to five years, so that the victory was a Pyrrhic one.

British unions conform to the American pattern of one-party government, the only exception being the small Association of

Draughtsmen, which has a two-party system. Apart from Communists and other radical groups, there are no permanent factions. There is more toleration of dissident groups than is true in the United States, although some unions have barred radicals from union office. Where there is no ideologically inspired opposition, there is likely to be little political life in an organization. To take the Transport Workers Union as an example, national elections are not hotly fought as a rule. Even at the district level, few workers know the candidates and their qualifications. Only at the branch level are there real contests.

There is much force in the recent assertion that the most important curb on British union leaders comes not from the constitution, but rather from the reluctance of members to give their leaders sufficient funds to run the organizations properly.[18] Union dues have lagged far behind wages and prices. Whereas average weekly earnings rose by 245 per cent between 1938 and 1956, dues rose by only 31 per cent, on the average. In 1956, the value of all union funds amounted to less than one week's total earnings of all union members. Roberts has estimated that the number of full-time officers and staff in British unions is about 10,000, or one for every 900 members, compared with 55,000, one for every 300 members, in the United States. This parsimonious attitude weakens union leadership, but it has also contributed to the failure of the branches to widen their functions sufficiently to curb the growth of unofficial shop stewards' movements.

TRADE UNIONS AND THE INDIVIDUAL

The problem of union security versus the right of the individual to refrain from joining a union has not aroused the same degree of passion in Britain as the "right to work" fight in the United States. However, the issue has been coming to the fore within the past five years, partly as a consequence of several important court decisions. It may well become of greater political moment in the future.

Union security clauses are not commonly found in British collective agreements, and as a result it is often thought that neither the closed nor the union shop is practiced. The TUC and its

---

[18] John A. Mack, "Trade Union Leadership," *The Political Quarterly*, Vol. XXVII (January–March, 1956), p. 76.

affiliates are officially opposed to the legal closed shop on the ground that if union membership is made compulsory by government sanction, then the government has an implied right to control conditions of membership and to police internal union affairs. Bred in a century of antipathy to regimes which were often hostile and rarely friendly, the unions still retain a reluctance to countenance government intervention, in spite of the rise of the Labour party. On the other hand, the TUC is no more enamored of the "free rider" than is the AFL–CIO, and many of its constituent organizations are committed in practice to 100 per cent unionism.

In some industries, this goal has been attained; among them are printing, longshore work, shipbuilding, mining, and music and the arts. Engineering, building and construction, and iron and steel are union-shop–prone industries, in which the union shop has been achieved in many, but not all, sections. There are some quasi-closed shop industries, in which management strongly encourages unionism. This is particularly true of the nationalized industries, road haulage and electric power being examples. There is no national closed shop in the latter, but workers in some areas have refused to work with nonunionists, making necessary the transfer of the recalcitrants. Finally, there are open-shop areas with closed-shop enclaves; distribution is generally nonunion, but the coöperatives are completely organized as a matter of principle. About 20 per cent of all British trade union members are in comprehensively closed- or union-shop areas, whereas 50 per cent in all are in wholly or partly closed industries.

There are no legal restrictions on either the closed or the union shop in Great Britain. A written or tacit agreement to limit employment to union members is perfectly lawful. However, pressure for complete unionization comes from the shop rather than from the union. Most union leaders are willing to concede that the man who is forced to join is not a reliable striker, that he may be the focus of disaffection, and that membership apathy may be a consequence of compulsory unionism. But to the man in the shop the "free rider" is anathema, and when he demands 100 per cent unionism there is little the union can do but back the demand.

The drive for the union shop is usually greatest where a high degree of unionization already prevails. In automobile plants, for example, the shop stewards will conduct a card check periodically, and if they find workers whose union standing is not in good order they will give them a week to pay their dues. If at the end of the waiting period this has not been done, and management refuses to discharge the nonunionists, short unofficial strikes are called to hamper operations. Once the union shop has been achieved, the shop is "registered" by oral agreement with management, which means that only union members in good standing can work there.

In spite of intense local pressure, there have been fairly numerous instances in which workers have refused to join or continue in unions. Where shop stewards are lax in collecting dues, or in going after new men, and large amounts of back dues accumulate, the amount of payment required to attain good standing may be quite substantial. The persistent lapser and the persistent evader have been the cause of most trouble.

Members of some religious sects—such as the Plymouth Brethren—have insisted on exemption from the obligation to join unions. There is no uniform solution to this problem. If the instance is an isolated one, and the man involved makes no fuss, he may be either ignored or asked to pay into a welfare fund in lieu of dues. But if he is militantly antiunion, and attempts to proselytize against the union, his discharge will be forced.

Finally, there are those who refuse to join for purely personal reasons—because they have had a row with the shop steward, disagree with union policy, or simply do not like unions. This group is the one which is the particular object of union antipathy.

The problem has been highlighted recently by several important court decisions. The leading case, *Bonsor* v *The Musicians' Union* (1955), involved a musician who was expelled by his branch secretary for falling fifty-two weeks in arrears on payment of his dues. When he was offered employment on condition that he regain his good standing, he applied for reinstatement, promising that he would pay his back dues out of his earnings. The union refused the offer, insisting that he pay all his arrears first. Thus unable to secure a musical position, he sued the union, and was awarded damages in a case that went as far as the House of Lords, the supreme judicial body of Britain. The basis for the decision was a rather narrow one: that under the constitution of the union, only the branch committee—not the branch secretary—was empowered to expel a member. However, the decision made it clear that the courts were going to force unions to follow their rules meticulously where individual membership rights were involved.

The impact of the *Bonsor* case was fortified by *Huntley* v *Thornton*, decided two years later. This involved a strike called by the Amalgamated Engineering Union in 1953. Huntley, a member of the union, refused to strike on the ground that the union had not followed its rules in the manner in which the strike had been called. His fellow employees "sent him to Coventry," refused to associate with him, and tried—unsuccessfully—to secure his discharge. The branch voted to ask the district committee to expel him, and this committee, in turn, recommended his expulsion to the national executive council, which had the exclusive right to take such action. However, the council refused to expel Huntley. Nevertheless, under the strain of his ostracism, Huntley finally left his job and secured employment eighty miles from his home. After two weeks of commuting, he decided to look for work nearer home, but the union district committee had notified all shop stewards in the area that he was to be boycotted. He finally secured a job at a near-by power station, but within two weeks he was dismissed after the shop steward had threatened to close the plant. Huntley then tried to make his peace with the union, offering to pay up all the dues which had accumulated while he was out of work. But this offer was refused, and he was expelled for nonpayment of dues. After working intermittently at odd jobs for another year, he finally secured a permanent position at an admiralty installation. He then brought suit against the union for the earnings he had lost, and was awarded £500 damages. The court held that the Trade Disputes Act of 1906, which bars suits against unions for acts committed in furtherance of a labor dispute, was not applicable since the action of the district committee was in the nature of a personal vendetta against Huntley rather than a labor dispute.

The informed legal consensus is that these cases provide only a limited degree of protection to individuals, and that they cannot be generalized much beyond their factual settings.[19] However, British unions are extremely sensitive to the mood of the courts, and many of them have hurried to shore up their practices against legal attack. Local unions have been directed to refrain from persecuting members, particularly men who have refused to join strikes. Union leaders have come out strongly against "sending men to Coventry." The new tone reflects the urgent desire of British unionism to keep clear of the courts. This is the traditional British way of doing things; instead of the unions being hit over

---

[19] See Cyril Grunfeld, "Trade Unions and the Individual: A Study of Recent Developments in England," *Journal of Public Law,* Vol. 7, No. 2 (1958), 289.

the head with a statutory club, they have been given a polite hint to mend their ways.

Apart from occasional lapses such as those involved in the *Bonsor* and *Huntley* cases, the internal judicial machinery of British trade unions seems to work reasonably well. Even before the *Bonsor* case, the courts had usually required that discipline be enforced strictly according to the rule book and that the rules provide for "natural justice."[20] Even strong critics of unionism have conceded that "the bodies at union headquarters to which appeal lies are, so far as we have been able to discover, usually well conducted."[21]

The customary channel of appeals in disciplinary cases is through the district office to the national executive. Of a sample of ninety-eight unions examined in a recent study, thirty-one permitted no appeal beyond the national executive. Forty others permitted the defendant to appeal to the delegate conference. Seven allowed appeal by referendum, although the process by which the referendum could be invoked was usually arduous in order to prevent frivolous appeal. Three unions had lay general councils to which appeal might be taken; nine had special appeals courts. Finally, eight union constitutions provide for outside arbitration as a last resort.

The Iron, Steel and Kindred Trades Association, for example, requires its executive council to select a panel of arbitrators, all of whom must be trade unionists from other organizations. A board of three arbitrators is selected from this panel: one by the appealing member, one by the executive council, and the third jointly by the other two.[22] However, no British union has adopted an external public review board procedure. The strong belief among trade unionists that outside interference in union affairs is to be avoided at all costs militates against this device.

Although review machinery, when invoked, seems to be adequate in most instances of victimization of individuals, the higher levels of the union rarely become involved. Most men who are expelled or otherwise penalized do not bother to appeal. In the General and Municipal Workers' Union, the second largest in the country, appeals to the national general council never total more

---

[20] Horatio Vester and Anthony H. Gardner, *Trade Union Law and Practice*, (London: Sweet & Maxwell, 1958), pp. 172–182.

[21] *A Giant's Strength: A Study by the Inns of Court Conservative and Unionist Society* (London: Christopher Johnson, 1958), p. 23.

[22] V. L. Allen, *Power in Trade Unions* (London: Longmans, 1954), pp. 164–170.

than three or four a year. With the pressures for conformity coming from below, greater union democracy at the grass roots level, and less union restraint of informal action in the shop, may thus lead to restriction rather than expansion of the protection afforded individuals.

A number of suggestions have been made for improving internal procedures. An obvious one is that a sentence of expulsion ought not to become effective until the exhaustion of appeals, to protect the employment of the accused. Another is that the TUC should set up an independent tribunal to which any aggrieved union member might appeal. It is unlikely, however, that these and other suggestions will be adopted in the near future. British unions are much less conscious than American unions of the force of public opinion. They are fairly immune from political attack, since the Conservative party is chary of challenging them in the absence of a much more aroused electorate than exists now. Only adverse court decisions are likely to have any impact upon their attitudes toward the rights of the individual.

COMPETITION AMONG UNIONS

Ever since its establishment, the TUC has occupied a unique position as the British trade union center. There was never the challenge to its monopoly status that the AFL faced on numerous occasions. Yet there has always been fairly keen competition among British unions for members. This stems from the fact that the principles of exclusive jurisdiction and majority rule in representation are not followed in Britain. Rival union raiding—or poaching, as it is termed—has been fairly common. Multiple unionism within single bargaining units is the rule rather than the exception.

This is not to say that raiding is accepted with equanimity. The Webbs inveighed against it more than half a century ago, and the TUC has been much concerned with the matter. The most recent instrument of control is the Bridlington Agreement, a resolution adopted by the 1939 congress of the TUC. Every union is now required to secure from each prospective member information relative to his previous union experience, and to refuse to admit a member of another union who is under discipline, engaged in a labor dispute, or delinquent in his dues. Nor may a union attempt to organize a shop in which a majority of the workers are represented by another union without permission of the latter.

Through the years, the TUC disputes committee has taken an increasingly stiff attitude toward transfers between unions. For example, in 1942, the National Union of Municipal Workers had enrolled 98 per cent of the workers in a certain plant, but subsequently lost its majority as a result of local differences. Between 1944 and 1945 the Chemical Workers' Union accepted some non-unionists in the plant, only to be rapped over the knuckles by the disputes committee for poaching. It is worth quoting some of the conclusions reached in a careful study of this interunion disputes mechanism:

The net result of the various changes in the T.U.C.'s principles for settling jurisdictional disputes . . . has been that *not a single post-war award has permitted transfers.* Although a worker has in principle the right to shift his union affiliation, the exercise of this right has grown so circumscribed by institutional sanctions that in practice he has not been able to transfer *if his union objected.* The T.U.C.'s premise has become that a union's right to retain its members is supreme over the member's right to change his affiliation in all cases in which the two come in conflict.

Most awards tend to benefit the big unions; these are the ones which have the greatest areas of organizing rights and which are able to grow by recruiting more *intensively* in those places where they have established these rights. Consequently, they have little need to infringe the jurisdictional claims of other unions. In practice, however, they frequently behave as though they are not interested in further expansion; few of them have carried out any important, large-scale organizing drives in the past ten years, but instead, they appear to be content with the *status quo.* The absence of inter-union competition appears to lead to sloth. But even large unions must prevent losses in membership to preserve the *status quo;* and, therefore, the major unions have developed a major interest in procedures which hinder inter-union mobility.

Many workers still believe in the principle of freedom of choice and are unwilling to have their exercise of this right sacrificed to the ideal of orderly inter-union relations; as a result, some members become non-unionists or apathetic while others revolt against their union. The prevalence of these problems which harm the trade union movement raises the question whether it is possible to establish orderly inter-union relations without violating the rights of members to join the union of their choice. If not, it is still arguable that the trade union movement has

63

gone too far in pursuit of the goal of orderly inter-union relations, and that more freedom of competition between unions would restrain bureaucracy and act as a healthy stimulus to recruitment.[23]

The Bridlington Agreement is not a binding contract at law, and the only means of enforcement is through expulsion of an offending union from the TUC. The courts have held that expulsion of a member from a union in accordance with an award of the TUC disputes committee was not lawful unless the union involved had a specific constitutional provision permitting such action. The TUC has recommended to its affiliates that they incorporate this authority in their statutes.

A closely related problem is that of the breakaway union. Usually a local group of workers withdraws to form an independent body. Both law and custom impose severe handicaps on such enterprises. It is well established that local union funds belong to the national union, so the seceding group must start with an empty treasury. More important, the employer need not bargain with the breakaway union, even if it represents a majority of his employees. This stems from the fact that there is no legally protected right of collective bargaining in Great Britain, as there is in the United States. A new group can win recognition only through its own efforts, and employers are understandably reluctant to incur the wrath of powerful, established unions by dealing with breakaways. The managing boards of the nationalized industries—particularly coal mining and dock work—tend to follow a policy of nonrecognition almost without exception. For example, the Stevedores' Union, a secession group from the Transport and General Workers, was refused recognition by the Dock Labor Board, and the bargaining claims of the Aeronautical Engineers' Association in the airlines were blocked by the Amalgamated Engineering Union.

There has been a trend in Britain toward larger organizational units and the growth of something like the concept of exclusive jurisdiction. This has been a matter of some concern so far as the effect is to reduce the worker's freedom of choice. B. C. Roberts writes, for example, that the traditionally untidy structures of British unions "whilst being a barrier to administrative efficiency, have played an important part in the maintenance of a democratic

---

[23] Shirley Lerner, "The T.U.C. Jurisdiction Disputes Settlement," *The Manchester School*, Vol. XXVI (September, 1958), 234, 235, 240.

system of union government and administration. There are considerable advantages to be obtained from the revision of the structure of trade union organization, but if it were to result in elimination of all competition between unions and the centralization of power in a few huge monopolistic organizations the gain in efficiency would be outweighed by the loss in democracy."[24] His recommendation, in the interest of American union democracy, that "union members should be able to vote with their feet as well as with their hands"[25] applies with equal force to Great Britain. A group of Conservative lawyers made the following recommendation: "When a genuine demand for a new union has shown itself by membership of a substantial proportion of a particular grade of workers being achieved and maintained for a considerable time that new union is morally entitled to recognition and it is in the long term interests of all that it should be recognized."[26] A writer in *The Economist* argued that "active poaching by trade unions—which means active competition among them—would not be a bad thing. It would, as in all other fields of endeavor, be a very good one."[27]

There are no immediate prospects for the growth of interunion competition in Britain. Rivalry violates the ethical precepts of the movement, which is still engrossed with unity in the face of a common foe—the employer. But there is a cultural lag involved here, for it has been many years since the existence of British unions has been threatened by any external enemy. When it is realized that competition can be permitted without any loss of bargaining power, the centripetal force that is now held in check by both organization and ideology—sectional dissatisfaction with bureaucratic leadership—may force greater tolerance of poaching and breakaways. There is sentiment for a more flexible policy not only outside, but within the labor movement as well.[28]

UNIONS AND POLITICS

The British Labour party began as a creature of the trade unions, and although it has since gained its independence, relations be-

---

[24] Roberts, *Trade Union Government*, p. 469.
[25] Roberts, *Unions in America*, p. 47. [26] *A Giant's Strength*, p. 46.
[27] *The Economist*, Vol. CLXXXVI (February 22, 1958), p. 639.
[28] See, for example, R. H. Crossman, *Socialism and the New Despotism*, Fabian Tract 298 (London: The Fabian Society, 1956).

tween the two branches of the labor movement remain close. Seventeen of the eighteen largest national unions are affiliated with the Labour party, and maintain political funds. The union member is subject to a political levy unless he specifically exempts himself by "contracting out" in writing, which he may do at any time.

The number of those who avail themselves of this opportunity varies greatly among unions. It seems, however, that many workers who vote Conservative do not bother to contract out. The Conservative party claims to have the support of 30 per cent of the workers, whereas the average contracting-out percentage is only about 10. These figures are not precisely matched, for workers who vote Conservative may belong to unions which are not affiliated with the Labour party. There is also the likelihood that many members of affiliated unions neither contract out nor pay the political levy. For example, I was told by the secretary of a branch of the Printers, Bookbinders and Paper Workers (a union with a relatively high proportion of contractors-out) that only 200 of 1,500 members actually pay the political levy, in spite of the fact that few had formally contracted out. Nevertheless, there must be many union members who are being taxed to support a political party which they oppose. Some unions follow the practice of discouraging contracting out by assessing those who do so an equal amount of money for other union purposes in order that contracting out shall carry no financial advantage.

One might think that this scheme would arouse a storm of protest, but in fact it is not much of an issue, particularly within the unions. The political levy is small, and many workers are probably unaware that they are paying it. If the amount were to be raised, there would almost certainly be an increase in contracting out. Substantial contracting-out percentages at present can usually be traced to the activities of militant anti-Labourites at the branch level. If someone takes the trouble to circulate the appropriate forms, there is an almost inevitable rise in the number of individuals who claim exemption. An exceptional instance is that of the Association of Engineering and Shipbuilding Draughtsmen, one of the few unions with any appreciable number of Conservative branch officials and in which a long battle over the political levy has resulted in reducing the number who pay to 45 per cent.

In return for their financial support, the trade unions have a large voice in the formulation of Labour party policy, both at the annual party congresses, where the trade union bloc vote is in the majority, and in Parliament. Many unions encourage selection of their officers as parliamentary candidates by offering to pay their election expenses, and by supplementing their parliamentary salaries if they are elected. It is an unwritten law in the Parliamentary Labour party that a certain proportion of its members must come from the trade unions. To neglect deserving trade union officials is to court financial disaster.

The Conservative party has organized trade union advisory councils in many districts, but its structure precludes party membership except individually through local constituency associations. However, even if it did permit collective affiliation, the trade union harvest would undoubtedly be very small. It is not fashionable, to put it mildly, for workers openly to support the Conservatives.

Yet a certain amount of doubt has been expressed about the wisdom of organic ties between the trade unions and the Labour party, and the Labour party defeat in the general elections of 1959 is bound to reinforce these doubts. From the trade union side, it is far less a matter of catering to the political views of minorities than the pragmatic question of whether unions could do better economically if they were politically neutral. Any British government must consult the trade unions on a great variety of problems, and if there are many more years of Conservative rule the attachment of workers to the idea that social justice can be attained only under a Labour government is bound to be weakened. The position that it is the better part of valor to have a foot in both campus will be strengthened.

On the other side, one hears the argument that a divorcement from the trade unions would not be an unmitigated calamity for the Labour party. It might be possible, then, to attract more white collar workers, who often vote as much against the unions, which they feel menace their economic interests, as against Labour party policy. To avoid the fate of becoming a permanent minority sect, the Labour party may be obliged to separate itself somewhat from the unions and seek to broaden its social base. The advocates of so drastic a policy are still few in number, but another electoral defeat could conceivably produce a major shakeup in the structure of British labor.

It is perhaps too much to say that British labor is facing a major crisis at the present time, except in the political sphere. But there are a good many thorny problems that will have to be faced if the trade unions are to retain their present degree of effectiveness.

The shop stewards, the unofficial strikes, and the drift of earnings beyond the contract level in many industries—the latter a partial consequence of the first two—flow essentially from the contradiction between a type of collective bargaining and union organization that suited a background of unemployment and the system and structures required for postwar full employment. Coupled with the age and hardening of the arteries of most British unions, making them almost incapable of change, this leaves a great deal unresolved at the workshop level. In the main, it is left to progressive managements, where they exist, to try to fill the institutional vacuum outside the nexus of employer associations or trade unions. If the British trade unions are to retain their traditional place as the main bulwark of the nation's industrial democracy, they will have to deal swiftly and explicitly with the twin problems of local union structure and local bargaining procedure.

SCANDINAVIA

The Scandinavian area includes three independent and distinctive nations (four if Finland, which is not covered in this study, is counted as a member of the Scandinavian bloc). Denmark, Norway, and Sweden are bound together by similarity in language and culture, but there are many differences among them as to specific institutional development, in response to variations in economic environment. Their trade union movements have borrowed a great deal from one another; yet the Norwegian and Swedish unions are based strictly on the principle of industrial structure, whereas Danish unionism is more like the British in that general and industrial unions exist side by side.

All three nations are alike in that the trade unions, in close alliance with the Labor or the Socialist parties, play a central, if not the decisive, role in their politics. The Labor parties of Norway and Sweden have ruled their respective countries, alone or as dominant partners in coalitions, uninterruptedly for a quarter of a century (except in Norway during the war). The Danish

Socialist party is relatively weaker, but it has been the senior partner in government coalitions for most of the postwar years. There are no religious or ethnic minority groups of any consequence to pose a threat to labor unity. Indeed, except for a small and dwindling Communist element, the workers of Scandinavia are almost without exception rallied behind their Social Democratic union leaders and their Labor parties.

LOCAL UNION ORGANIZATION

Scandinavian trade unions are based upon solid local organization. In this respect, they are more like American than British unions. There is no shop steward problem because the shop stewards and officials of the union are subject to union control. The best way to illustrate the contrast between local union structure in Scandinavia and in most of the rest of Europe is by a few examples.

One of the largest local unions in Denmark is a Copenhagen local of the Danish General Workers' Union which has jurisdiction over truck drivers, warehousemen, automobile service stations, and allied industries. Its 5,600 members are subdivided into forty shop clubs, ranging in size from eighteen to three hundred members each. The club elects an executive committee and one or more shop stewards by secret ballot. Shop stewards handle individual grievances and shop-contract disputes, under the supervision of the local's officers. The clubs hold occasional membership meetings, although they are not required to do so by union rule.

The local union itself has full-time officers, elected annually at general membership meetings. Once a man is elected, however, he is assured of reëlection until he resigns or retires. This does not mean that there is no opposition within the local, but simply that it does not take the form of rival slates for union office. The Communists, who constitute a small but persistent factional group, seem to regard this method of opposition as futile.

General membership meetings are held twice a year, but attendance is low, ranging between three hundred and five hundred. The real governing body is the general council, consisting of the four officers and five lay members, which meets every few weeks. In periods of crisis, however, membership participation increases sharply. Under the Danish collective bargaining system, all new agreements must be ratified by the workers covered; in advance of the referendum, this local, like most others, calls a meeting to discuss the provisions of the contract proposal. In 1958, about two thousand members attended the meeting, and most of the twenty-seven speakers were from the rank and file.

Although the DGWU does not have any union shop agreements, there is 100 per cent unionism within the jurisdiction of the local. It is simply taken for granted by both workers and employers that union membership is a condition of employment, and recalcitrants are discharged as a matter of routine. In spite of its strength, the local is concerned about membership apathy. It publishes a monthly news bulletin, sponsors art exhibits, theatrical performances, film shows, vacation trips, dances, and an ambitious educational program, but the leaders are frank in conceding that as yet they have found no way to counteract the lack of active participation on the part of most of their constituents.

A second example of Scandinavian structure is afforded by the 30,000 members of the Stockholm local of the Swedish Metal Workers' Union. Its size makes general membership meetings impracticable; instead there is a representative assembly of four hundred, meeting at least four times a year. The assembly is composed of delegates elected by 205 formally organized shop clubs, and two hundred less formal groups in the smaller enterprises. Each club is run by a shop committee, the chairman of which is usually the delegate to the representative assembly. Until 1950, when the Communists were strong in the local (they controlled it from about 1943 until 1948), there were many bitter contests for the shop chairmanship, but these are no longer in evidence.

Finally, there is the Oslo local of the Norwegian Municipal Workers' Union. A much smaller organization of 1,100, it is divided into six groups corresponding to the city administrations in which its members are employed, the chairman of each group being a member of the local executive committee. About 80 per cent of the eligible employees are organized, a few of the non-members belonging to a small independent union sponsored by the Conservative party.

The local holds four membership meetings a year, but as usual attendance is low, averaging only between fifty and seventy members. Group meetings are better attended, particularly when salary questions are being discussed. Each group is run by a nine-man executive committee, and each separate office elects a shop steward—of whom there are eighty—by secret ballot. The local has no full-time officers, and there is considerable rotation among the part-time people, since union office involves much work and no pay. However, a certain amount of power goes with the shop steward posts, since committees of shop stewards have authority to make recommendations for appointments and promotions. Although the city administration is not required to follow such recommendations, it usually does.

Norwegian municipal employees have the right to strike; in 1958 there was a three-day strike in Oslo, the first in thirty years. At the conclusion of the strike two hundred more employees joined the union, accounting for its largest membership increase in many years. The problem that this local faces, together with the rest of the Scandinavian unions, is how to keep its members interested without strikes.

These three unions, differing as they do in size and detail of organization, nevertheless have certain common characteristics that typify Scandinavian locals. There is not an enterprise with more than a few workers which does not have an elected shop steward. Even on temporary construction work, shop stewards are elected for the duration of the job. Members pay their dues as a matter of course, even without the checkoff, to which most of the unions are opposed in principle. The level of dues payment varies considerably, depending mainly upon the variety of welfare services which the union offers its members, but in all instances dues are adequate for a sound financial administration. Locals often retain a large share of the dues. The Copenhagen Transport and Warehouse Union, for example, keeps 70 per cent of the dues after deducting the part which goes into the union's unemployment fund. The Stockholm Metal Workers' Local has built up a treasury of $200,000, a large sum for Sweden.

Scandinavian collective bargaining is mainly industry-wide in scope, and this has contributed to a decline of local function. There are counteracting forces at work, however. Some industries—the metal trades in particular—employ the "minimum wage" system of payment, in which only minimum rates for the various skill categories are set by contract, leaving the determination of actual wage rates to individual bargaining between the workers and the employers. The unions have to keep an eye on the level of wages thus determined in order to prevent any shop from gaining a competitive advantage by bargaining out lower average wages.

In other instances, unions have deliberately attempted to restore policy functions to their locals. For example, when hours were recently reduced from forty-eight to forty-five per week by national agreement, some of the Danish and Swedish national unions left it up to their locals to work out the precise pattern of weekly hours although the national unions retained an advisory function. A diversity of solutions resulted, after much active discussion by members. The new Swedish law on working hours intentionally opens the way for local option on the number of weekly working hours, permitting workers to decide between income and leisure.

Scandinavian enterprises above a certain minimum size are obliged by law or agreement to establish labor-management committees. Their function is consultative rather than administrative; they are designed to educate workers in the economics of their industry and to provide a means of communication between management and labor, all in the interest of higher productivity. In general, these committees have fallen short of expectations. They have revolutionized neither labor nor management attitudes. Committee meetings have too often been concentrated on unimportant details, and neither side has had an adequate understanding of exactly what the committees are supposed to do. Particularly in Sweden, however, a real effort has been made by national unions and employer associations to train representatives for production committee work, and this may yet bear fruit.

The over-all picture of local unionism in Scandinavia is one of complete organization combined with declining membership interest. It is frequently said in Sweden that to the worker the union is a slot machine—he puts in his dues and expects a periodic wage increase in return.[29] Many explanations have been adduced

---

[29] A knowledgable Swedish friend, who has been active in the labor movement in Sweden, commented as follows on this statement: "Is this not too gloomy a picture? It is true that membership participation in meetings is low; why go to the meetings when nothing upsetting is in the cards? But this was always so. What amazes me is *how intense* the consciousness of the importance of unionism is among the rank and file in spite of the 'bureaucratic centralism' of wage bargaining. The local handling of piece rate negotiations and settling of cases of individual merit wages and various grievances means a lot, and this also explains a lot. One measure of interest, which is perhaps better than attendance at meetings, is the fact that a strike is always 100% when and if there is a strike. There is not the

to explain this phenomenon: rising living standards, the lack of clearly defined problems to be solved, the decline of political factionalism, the universality of unionism. Real effort is currently being made to find remedies, but thus far without success.

THE NATIONAL UNION AND THE FEDERATION

Salaries

Scandinavian union officers receive very moderate pay scales. National union officers in Sweden receive about 25,000 kronor per annum. (This is $5,000 at the official exchange rate, perhaps $8,000 in real value.) The average income of Stockholm industrial workers is 14,000 kronor, while Stockholm building workers earn from 15,000 to 22,000 kronor. There is no comparable uniformity in Denmark and Norway, but salaries are lower than in Sweden. As a result, union leaders in these countries remain workers in their style of living. They have neither United States incomes nor British titles to lift them out of the working class. Incidentally, such union technicians as engineers and economists often earn more than elected officials. Financial control of union funds is very tight, and corruption is non-existent.

Membership

Sweden, a country with about seven and a half million inhabitants, has about two million trade union members, of whom near one and a half million are in unions affiliated with the Swedish Federation of Labor, and the rest with the Central Organization of Salaried Employees. If the same proportion of American employees were unionized, there would be about forty million union members in the United States. The degree of organization is somewhat lower in Denmark and Norway, although still very high by any other comparative standard. The Danish Federation of Labor has 720,000 members from a population of four million; the Norwegian Federation of Labor, 550,000 from a population of three and a half million.

The organizational society *par excellence* of the Western world

---

slightest question of any strikebreaking. Also, the fact that membership is constantly increasing is a sign of vitality. How could you keep local committeemen on their toes persuading new employees to join if there were a declining sense of meaning in the work?"

is Sweden. Not only are most manual and white collar workers unionized, but professionals, civil servants, farmers, and employers are joined together in organizations designed to further their economic interests. Pluralism has strong economic roots; but in this land of competing interest groups, some are beginning to fear that the individual will be overlooked. The implication of a system of power blocs for individual rights is a matter of some public concern; but up to now, the emphasis has been upon perfection of organization to advance collective interests.

Leadership

Although the Swedish unions generally elect their officers for life, whereas the Norwegians and Danes require them to stand for reëlection periodically, there is little practical difference among the three countries—in each a union leader can expect to remain in office until he reaches the retirement age. However, a particularly able man will tend to be advanced more rapidly in his own union or move into the office of the federation. But the semicompulsory retirement age and the ubiquity of the "crown prince" system reduce the dangers inherent in the problem of succession: one need not play politics constantly in order to safeguard a union position.

There are strong, dominating personalities at the head of many Scandinavian unions, but power tends to be vested in national committees, most of which include lay members. The Swedish Metal Workers Union, for example, is governed by a congress of three hundred meeting quadrennially, a general council of thirty-three meeting at least twice a year, and an executive committee of nine meeting weekly. Of the general council members, fourteen are either members or alternate members of the executive committee; of the remaining nineteen, two are branch officers, and the rest at the bench. The executive committee consists of the four national officers and five lay members, with the five senior members of the secretariat serving as alternate members. The lay members of the general council and the executive committee are compensated for travel expenses and loss of working time, but they are not permitted to hold any other paid union office. By all accounts, these rank-and-file men have strong local backing, and are quite capable of standing up to the permanent officers. However, the executive committee rarely divides along officer–lay-

74

member lines. The officers usually come to meetings with proposals on which they have agreed among themselves, but modify them if they encounter any serious resistance from the lay members. Although the latter may not match the officers in their knowledge of industrial conditions, it was the view of all officers interviewed that the lay members performed exceedingly well. And as one officer put it, if members began to grumble, the officers can reply: "Your own fellows have a majority on the executive. Don't blame us." This pattern of the lay majority on executive boards is quite common in Scandinavia, and is regarded as an important contributor to union democracy.

Centralization of Decision-Making

Collective bargaining is much more centralized in Scandinavia than in the United States. The federations of labor play a far greater role than the AFL–CIO—or the British TUC—in formulating policy and in conducting negotiations. Increasingly, the pattern of bargaining has come to consist of a general agreement negotiated by the federation of labor and the employers' association, followed by its adaptation to specific industries by the national unions and employers concerned.

The building and construction industry is one in which we expect atomistic bargaining because of the nature of the product market. In Norway, however, the Building Workers' Union, an industrial organization including all the building trades except the bricklayers, negotiates a national agreement covering the whole country. Piece rates are uniform, though earnings tend to be higher in the large cities because work can be done more efficiently on larger projects. Owing to the force of federation policy, the wages of building workers have been kept down, on the theory that those working in sheltered markets should not be permitted to exploit the employees producing for foreign markets. Many building workers have been dissatisfied with this restriction upon their bargaining power, and if local option held sway, they would undoubtedly eliminate it. But thus far the national union has been able to contain the unrest, although at one time a Communist minority was able to capitalize upon the issue. Some of the union's leaders fear, however, that eventually this policy may lead to a weakening of the national union's authority.

The lines of communication between union and member are

probably better developed in Scandinavia than anywhere in the world. Not only are there the customary union journals, but there is a well-developed labor press that competes with commercial newspapers. The daily trade union newspaper in Stockholm has a circulation of 170,000 in the morning and 200,000 in the evening, about half that of the city's largest papers. In addition, there are about thirty other labor papers scattered throughout the country. The Norwegian labor press is, if anything, more successful than the Swedish, but the Danish labor press is somewhat weaker. It is a sign of the times that the Copenhagen labor press recently changed its name from *Social Demokraten* (*The Social Democrat*) to *Aktuelt* (*The News*), in order to hold its dwindling circulation. There is also, in all three countries, a remarkable system of workers' education, replete with modern residence schools, which reaches a large part of the membership. Through these means of communication, the Scandinavian worker has been given an excellent education in the economics of his country and his industry, which has facilitated the successful execution of policies calling for a large measure of individual coöperation and restraint.

The Referendum

The referendum has long been employed in Scandinavian trade union government. In Denmark, the constitutions of most unions still require the ratification of new agreements by referendum. However, through the years it was found that since only about half of those eligible to vote cast ballots, organized minorities were often able to frustrate the consummation of agreements hammered out by the leaders. But so strong was tradition that leadership dared not go directly to the rank and file with a proposal to abolish the referendum. Instead, a law was passed by a Socialist government which stipulated that when a single union was covered by a proposed contract, rejection by a majority of those voting was valid only if at least 75 per cent of those eligible to vote participated; and that for each percentage point by which participation fell below 75, the majority necessary for rejection was increased by one-half of one percent. Where agreements covered more than one union—as is more usual—the deficit of votes below 75 per cent of the eligibles could be cast en bloc by the representative assembly. These rules have made it unlikely that a contract approved by the leadership will be defeated in a referendum.

The Swedish unions, which are much more adverse to government interference in their affairs than the Danish, tackled the problem more directly. The 1941 congress of the federation of labor adopted a resolution by which all affiliated national unions were required to amend their constitutions to the effect that referenda could be advisory only, leaving the final decisions to national executive committees. The Norwegian unions, by a combination of legislation and agreement with the employers' association, have made it difficult, though still possible, to upset agreements by referenda.

The referendum became popular after 1918, when the labor movements had become radicalized under the influence of the Russian Revolution and the political turmoil that affected all Europe. Its decline as a decision-making mechanism stems from its fundamental inconsistency with any coördination or systematic planning of wage policy on an industry-wide or economy-wide scale. Where many conflicting interests are delicately balanced, it becomes intolerable to permit one union to upset an agreement and jeopardize the industrial peace of an entire nation.

Although on the surface, the referendum seems to be an ideal instrument for democratic decision-making, there are many drawbacks to its effective employment. The principal one is the failure of a large part of the electorate to vote, thus giving dedicated minority groups influence far beyond their numerical strength. In union terms, the further one moves away from the local bargaining unit, the less satisfactory is the referendum as a means of eliciting membership opinion. One may question the wisdom, from a democratic viewpoint, of all-embracing bargaining units. But given a system of national bargaining, the mandatory referendum simply will not work. Its use as an advisory mechanism is useful, however, for no leadership can long afford to act against membership majorities, no matter how those majorities were secured.

Other Aspects of National Union Government

National unions in the Scandinavian countries do not have the authority to put local unions in receivership; they may only expel. Naturally, this weapon is used with extreme caution. For a number of years, the two largest locals of the Swedish Metal Workers, in Stockholm and Gothenburg, were controlled by Communists, who were doing their very best to embarrass the national office. The national union, instead of "reorganizing" the locals, relied upon slow rank-and-file action to eliminate the Communists from leadership positions, a much more difficult, but in the end more satisfactory, solution.

One particularly interesting practice found in many Scandinavian unions is the right of any local union, shop club, or individual member to present a resolution for action at the national union congress. The national executive may indicate its approval or disapproval, but the resolution must be printed in the agenda and submitted to a vote. Of the 120 resolutions that came before the last congress of the Swedish Metal Workers' Union, five were sponsored by individual members. As a practical matter, such resolutions have little chance unless they are approved by the national executive, but there is some point in having every member know that his ideas will be considered by the highest legislative body of his union.

THE UNION AND THE INDIVIDUAL

Compulsory union membership by collective agreement is seldom to be found in Scandinavia. The employers' associations have consistently refused to permit their members to enter into agreements containing any form of union security clause. Thus, it is only with an occasional unorganized employer that unions sign such contracts. However, many employers, including those who belong to the employers' associations, follow closed- or union-shop procedure as a matter of policy. A recent volume by Allan Rise, the managing director of the Danish Employers' Association, explains:

. . . at the present time, with the extremely high organizational percentage of workers in the country, the right to employ unorganized workers is mainly of theoretical interest. One may say that it is the general opinion among employers to confine themselves to the use of organized workers, partly to avoid unrest in the shop and partly to have the union to turn to if the individual worker does something which entitles the employer to complain. But the Employers' Association continues to prevent its members from entering into so-called "exclusive agreements," i.e., agreements to employ organized workers only, arising from its principled opposition to employers acting as whips for the union.[30]

If there is an occasional worker who refuses to join a union, he may be boycotted, or the employer may be warned to discharge him on threat of a strike. A few people with religious scruples are permitted to remain outside the unions, though only after an examination to determine whether this is the motivating cause.

Since there is complete unionization in a large part of the labor market (retail trade, farming, lumbering, and road haulage are somewhat less well organized), the protection of individual rights is of crucial importance—workers who run afoul of the unions may find their employment opportunities severely limited. For example, under the statutes of the Swedish federation of labor, which are binding on all affiliated unions, no worker can be denied admission to the union with jurisdiction over his trade unless there is some circumstance which would warrant his expulsion if he were a member. Most unions stipulate expulsion for failing to pay dues for eight weeks, for action as a strikebreaker, or for other serious breaches of union discipline.

The Swedish Supreme Court and the special Labor Court have insisted that disciplinary procedure must conform strictly to the union constitution. Thus, a man who was expelled from a local union for refusing to participate in an illegal strike was ordered reinstated with compensation for lost wages. In another case, a member of the Metal Workers' Union was expelled because he introduced a motion at a local meeting to the effect that the local should disregard a national union circular banning Communists from union office, exclusion being based on a constitutional provision requiring members to comply with national union decisions. The courts held the expulsion unlawful because the constitution did not clearly specify that this was an offense warranting such discipline.

Generally speaking, only the national executive committee has the right to expel, with appeal going to the general council and to the congress. The executive committee may commute a recommendation for expulsion to loss of the right to hold union office, with no further reduction of membership rights, a form of discipline that has been used in political instances. A number of

---

[30] Allan Rise and Jens Degerbøl, *Grundregler i Dansk Arbejdsrett* (*Basic Rules of Danish Labor Law*) (Copenhagen: Nyt Nordisk Forlag, 1959), p. 77.

unions have banned Communists from union office, but have never excluded them as a class. Even at the present time when Communist strength has fallen greatly, their number would make exclusion impractical.

Swedish union members have the right by union constitution to appeal disciplinary action taken by the local union (including a recommendation for expulsion) to arbitration. The arbitration committee consists of two members designated by the local union, two by the appellant, with the chairman chosen jointly by these four; if they cannot agree, the chairman is designated by the national executive committee. Thus far, the general counsel of the Federation of Labor has served as chairman in most instances, but the present general counsel feels that the chairman of the Labor Court would be a more appropriate chairman and hopes that this will be the future pattern.

There have been only a dozen arbitration cases in the twenty-five years this provision has been in effect. Most of these were lost by the appellants. In general, they involved personal rather than political issues, and some of the individuals were mentally unbalanced. There might have been more cases were there not a deterrent to litigation in the fact that the arbitration committee can assess costs against the appellant. Nonetheless, the possibility of arbitration is of basic importance in the protection of the individual against arbitrary union action. It should be noted that there is no comparable right in either Denmark or Norway.

There is little discussion of this whole range of issues in contemporary Scandinavia. Most informed persons consider existing safeguards to be adequate, given the accepted social norm of the desirability of union membership. Union security has not been a live issue for many years, because the unions are regarded as almost quasi-governmental bodies. Because of this fact, the question of internal union democracy becomes much more critical, and will probably occasion livelier concern in the future.

UNIONS AND POLITICS

As already indicated, Scandinavian trade unions are closely allied with political parties which cater mainly, if not exclusively, to the working class. This alliance takes the form of collective affiliation by local unions in Norway and Sweden. About half the party membership is based upon collective affiliation. There is provision for contracting out by union members who are opposed to the Labor party, but there are no over-all data on the number of persons who avail themselves of this privilege. Few objections have been raised, however, except when the Communists were strong. In the Swedish Railwaymen's Union, for example, where there are few Communists, between 40 and 50 per cent of the locals voted to affiliate with the Social Democratic party, and only eighty or ninety of the 1,600 members in Stockholm contracted out. The Stockholm Metal Workers' local, in which the Communists have been strong, registered 3,500 objectors of 30,000 members. In this local, even when a man contracts out, he continues to pay the political levy, but he can have it refunded in a lump sum at the end of the year; and although about 10 per cent contract out, only 1 per cent of the members ever come to collect their payments. It is obviously the principle, not the cash, that is important to them. Collective trade union affiliation is not practiced in Denmark.

All three countries have joint trade-union–labor-party committees to coördinate policy.[31] Both national and local unions give financial support to the Labor parties out of regular dues funds, in addition to the political levy, a practice which is entirely legal. These funds must usually be voted in each separate instance, and as a result, trade union leaders have considerable influence in party councils. The threat to withhold funds can be a potent one, since union donations constitute the main source of election money. Trade union leaders sit in Parliament, and are often allotted those cabinet posts of most interest to them, such as the departments handling public works, social security, and the determination of civil service salaries. Union leaders who serve in the cabinet are required to relinquish their union posts.

There is much less controversy within the Scandinavian labor movement than in Britain over the desirability of a close alliance

---

[31] A well-informed Swede put the question of coördination in the following terms, which I think summarize the matter neatly for all Scandinavia: "In practice, the official committee, at least in Sweden, does not mean very much. Coordination is much more a matter of personal contact and mutual understanding without many words. Sometimes unity on means and short term tactics has not been great; think of the open disagreement on wage policy in 1952 and 1955, and tax policies in several cases during the fifties. Actually, coordination to a great extent has taken the form of putting before one another *faits accomplies* which are then (grumblingly) accepted by the other party in order to avoid spectacular public displays of disunity. LO accepts (with some critical comments) the government's 'jurisdiction' over politics; and the government (often with deep sorrow) LO's jurisdiction over wage policies."

between unions and party. After all, the Scandinavian labor parties have been eminently successful, and it can be argued with considerable justification that the gains achieved by workers through their control of the state have been fully as important as those secured through collective bargaining. As long as the labor parties hold their positions, few voices are likely to be raised against their support by the unions.

The opposition parties are unhappy about this arrangement, and are constantly questioning the morality of using dues money for partisan politics. But they simply lack the power either to legislate against the practice or to attack it from within the unions. In the Copenhagen General Workers' transport local, for example, a recent resolution to withhold funds from the Socialist party received the support of only twenty-seven of the four hundred members attending the meeting. Except for a few Communists, non-Socialist local or shop chairmen are oddities.

From 1945 until about the time of the uprising in Hungary, the Communist party had substantial strength in the Scandinavian trade unions.[32] It controlled a number of local unions and a few national unions as well. There were rival political caucuses at many union congresses, and even leadership contests. But a Socialist offensive and the vagaries of Soviet foreign policy have since combined substantially to reduce Communist influence. In Denmark, for example, the veteran general secretary of the Communist party, Aksel Larsen, was expelled from the party for refusing to condone the Russian attack on Hungary, and took with him most of the Communist trade union activists.

There is in Sweden a syndicalist trade union center, but it has only 17,000 members, and has no influence in the country. The Communists have not been replaced by any political opposition, and the result is a noticeable decline in political interest within the unions. There is no membership raiding among the standard unions, and an occasional jurisdictional dispute is handled firmly by the parent federation. Once in a while, an independent union group will emerge as a consequence of some local fight, but a breakaway union has no chance of survival.

In present-day Scandinavia, therefore, a trade union movement has achieved the goal sought by trade unions the world

---

[32] In Sweden, they were at the height of their influence in 1945, but lost ground steadily thereafter.

over. Organization is practically complete, rival unionism is nonexistent, and internal differences have diminished almost to the vanishing point. Through closely allied political parties, unions have a considerable degree of control of their governments. Collective bargaining has become an aspect of economic planning, and the strike weapon is growing rusty with disuse. But success has its price; with no worlds left to conquer, and with further improvements in material standards dependent entirely on the slow growth of productivity, to which unions can contribute little, workers may be losing interest in the organization to which they were so strongly devoted in the past.

The more forward-looking of the union leaders have come to the realization that the survival of their organizations as vital social institutions implies an expansion of function beyond the traditional areas of union activity. And it is a hopeful sign that they are beginning to explore the possibility of unionism as a force for augmenting the scope of individual, as well as collective action. Within the past few years, there has been an interesting debate within the Swedish labor movement on the desirability of increasing labor mobility, not only within local labor markets and geographically, but among occupations and industries as well, in order to give workers more freedom of choice among jobs.[33] In other words, more stress is being laid on creating liberty, security, and economic welfare for the individual by helping him adapt himself to changing economic conditions and personal desires, than upon reliance on measures which improve wages and other conditions on the spot where the individual happens to be. Measures of the latter variety are often exclusive in character, giving benefits to a certain group at the cost of creating rigidities. There are those within the labor movement who feel that the government should act much more vigorously to help the worker overcome obstacles to movement into the better-paying industries.

It is too early to say what will come of these and similar suggestions. There are many who regard them as visionary and impractical. But it may be that here again, as in the past, Scandinavia will serve as a social laboratory for the western world.

---

[33] See in particular, Gosta Rehn, "Reformistisk fornyelse," *Tiden,* Nos. 3 and 4 Vol. 51 (1959), pp. 135, 196.

SWEDISH WHITE COLLAR UNIONISM

One feature of the Swedish labor scene that cannot be passed by without special note is the remarkable union organization of white collar workers. The Central Organization of Salaried Employees (TCO) is an independent federation with 350,000 members in thirty-six affiliated unions. The federation of labor, in addition, has 150,000 members in the lower salary grades of the railroads, the post office, and municipal government.

The TCO is a relatively new organization, with an aggressive leadership. About half its members are in private industry, the other half in civil service, county, and municipal employment. TCO members are much less politically homogeneous than manual workers; perhaps a third of its number are Socialists, and the rest support either the Conservative or the Liberal party. Political neutrality has consequently been a *sine qua non* for successful organization, although TCO officials are free to participate in politics, and are even encouraged to do so, as individuals.

The largest of the TCO unions is the Swedish Union of Clerical and Technical Employees in Industry (SIF) with a membership of 100,000. Within its ranks there are chief engineers, construction executives, designers, work study engineers, draftsmen, accountants, sales managers, salesmen, stenographers, typists, and telephone operators. The only industrial white collar employees not eligible for membership are managing directors and department heads. Some ten SIF locals have full-time officers; the rest are manned by part-time personnel. Although top staff members do not dominate the union, engineers are overrepresented in governing bodies. Although attendance at local meetings is typically low, there is a much more lively interest within the 1,500 shop clubs, mainly because it is at this level that bargaining is carried on. There are no uniform national or even local salary scales, each office constituting a separate bargaining unit, but the parent organization collects salary statistics to assist the local bargainers. SIF has a large strike fund, but it has only been drawn upon three times since the organization's founding in 1920, though economic warfare is by no means out of the question. In 1955, a lockout by the Metal Trades Employers' Association against 35,000 SIF members, arising out of a strike threat to one employer, was narrowly averted. Like TCO, SIF is politically neutral. Its executive board includes four Conservatives, three Liberals, and two Socialists.

The Federation of Civil Servants, with 22,000 members, 12,000 of them women, is the largest civil service affiliate of TCO. Swedish civil servants have no statutory right to bargain collectively, though government agencies do bargain with them as a customary matter. There is no right of strike; on occasion, however, the unions have "blockaded" government agencies by preventing the entry of new personnel. The federation caters mainly to the lower salary categories, but it numbers among its members state governors and ambassadors.

Among the other TCO unions are the Nurses Union, the Union of Non-Commissioned Officers in the Defense Forces, the Union of Policemen, and the Foremen's and Supervisors' Union. It is estimated that nurses, teachers, and army officers are completely organized; employees of private industry, about 85 per cent. Only in trade and commerce, where organization embraces from 40 to 50 per cent of the salaried labor force, is there any substantial nonunion sector left.

TCO unionism is effective by any standard. Relative white collar wages have been maintained in recent years, and even the government follows a "market wage" policy which takes not only union contracts but the "wage drift" above union-bargained rates into account. The TCO is affiliated with the International Confederation of Free Trade Unions, the only white collar federation to enjoy this status.

White collar workers are usually regarded as poor union material. There are many white collar unions outside Sweden, but nowhere else—not even in the other Scandinavian countries—is there anything approaching a counterpart of TCO.[34] Why Swedish employees have been willing to join unions is not at all clear; the fact is simply taken for granted. Among the elements that seem worthy of inquiry are the following: the fact that organization has taken place independently of the traditional manual unions; the high degree of organization among manual workers; the emphasis upon bargaining at the shop, rather than at the local or national union level; political neutrality; reasons for the accept-

---

[34] A possible exception is Austria, where a high proportion of white collar employees belong to the Austrian Federation of Labor.

ance by top management of organization by management personnel.

White collar unionism in Sweden is the most rapidly growing sector of the Swedish labor movement, and if it merely keeps pace with employment trends its relative importance is bound to increase. In many ways it is also the most vital and least bureaucratic part of the union movement—the one in which members participate most directly. As a portent of things to come in other nations, it is worthy of more attention than it has received.

CHAPTER IV. CONCLUSIONS

The value of comparative analysis lies largely in the light that it throws on the institutions of one's own society. We are so accustomed to certain ways of doing things that it is hard for us to conceive of alternatives. A knowledge of how other people live and work helps provide detachment and objectivity. It is necessary, however, to avoid the danger of advocating change too glibly on the basis of the "lessons" of other nations. A set of human institutions becomes adapted to a unique environment by a process of trial and error. The process of cultural borrowing, which goes on all the time, is not one of literal transplantation. A practice which works perfectly in one society may be completely irrelevant to another. It is with this cautionary note that we proceed to a consideration of the generalizations that emerge from the foregoing pages.

TRADE UNION PLURALISM

The most challenging problem encountered in the course of this study was that of unitary versus plural unionism. The French and Italian experience illustrates clearly how dangerous internal division can be to a labor movement which has not gained general acceptance. When trade unions are still in their fighting stage, when collective bargaining is impossible because of gross inequalities in bargaining power, and when industrial enterprises are run as autocracies, such concepts as trade union democracy and membership rights have little meaning. Unions are regarded by the workers who are not intimidated or indifferent as the spearhead of their drive for a voice in the determination of the conditions under which they work. Schism, even where fundamental differences in religion and political ideology prevail, becomes the cardinal sin: treason to the working class. Dissenting individuals or groups are strongly resented. The strength of Italian and French Communists in the trade unions stems from the fact that they captured the traditional trade union centers, and have played on the themes of legitimacy and unity in the face of a common employer foe with telling effect.

This same theme of insecurity has sometimes been invoked to justify undemocratic union practices in the United States. The late William Leiserson said:

Anyone who follows the speeches and public statements of union leaders must be impressed by their emphasis on threats to the security of the organizations. While leaders may stimulate such fears for their own advantage, the fact is that the membership by and large shares the feeling of apprehension for the safety of their organization. . . . It is in this feeling of insecurity that the explanation of undemocratic trends in union government must be sought. Autocratic practices of union officials would not be tolerated to the extent of alarming the friends of organized labor, members would hardly be willing to grant arbitrary powers to their executives and support or approve those who assume such power, were it not for the persistent fears that their unions were in danger of destruction or weakening to the point of ineffectiveness. From this feeling of insecurity stems the belief, common to rank and file and union officers alike, that unity of labor is the all-important consideration, that dissenters, whether member or nonunion worker, endanger the existence of the unions and the industrial governments they force on employers.[1]

---

[1] William M. Leiserson, *American Trade Union Democracy* (New York: Columbia University Press, 1959), pp. 69–70.

In the Low Countries, and in Scandinavia, Austria, and Great Britain, trade unions have gained unassailable positions. An employer there who conceives of the possibility of a nonunion society is an impractical dreamer. Union leaders may on occasion unfurl the red banners of the working class against capitalist exploitation, but everyone understands that this is part of the collective bargaining game.

In these circumstances, competition among unions has an altogether different significance. Here, it may act as a powerful lever for the furtherance of internal union democracy. The union cannot take its members for granted—they may walk out without shame or fear. It is no longer sufficient, for holding their allegiance, to produce periodic economic gains, since competing organizations are bound by the nature of the bargaining system to produce equivalent gains.

Pluralism in the Low Countries is largely the product of a religious and political cleavage that runs vertically throughout society. To some extent, unions do have a captive membership, for an ardent Catholic in Holland will not risk excommunication by joining a Socialist-oriented union. However, membership is by no means automatic, for not only do many workers have a real choice, but there is always the nonunion option, since the union shop is unknown. Unions must therefore justify themselves to their members and to the public as organizations which are rendering an essential service through democratic means. Union government cannot be wrapped in secrecy on the ground that to reveal its inner workings would be to play into the hands of employers. Union officials are held to the same degree of accountability in handling other people's money as are public officials. There cannot be the double morality which condones the stuffing of union ballot boxes in the interest of efficiency and condemns dishonesty in political elections, for union efficiency in bargaining is no longer that important. The threshold of tolerance for autocratic union government becomes much lower where leaders can no longer don the garb of crusaders.

We must guard against any erroneous postulation of a necessary one-to-one relationship between union democracy and union rivalry. Neither the British nor the Scandinavian unions are run in despotic fashion, in spite of the absence of worker choice. But in this group of nations, the price of monopoly seems to be a disquieting growth of membership apathy, and a noticeable loosening of the ties between workers and unions. There are many in these countries who think that affording workers greater freedom of membership would go a long way toward putting the unions on their mettle.

Can it be said that trade unions in the United States have attained a sufficiently high degree of security so that competition among them would act as a liberating influence rather than endanger their existence? To quote Leiserson once more:

The strength of organized labor is not lessened by its divisions. Split into two main centers in 1936, the AFL and the CIO together had doubled union membership four or five years later. In another five years, the total membership in all organizations including independent unions had tripled. . . . Unions raid each other for members; by means of government-conducted elections they contest each other's right to represent employees and bargain for them. Such interunion rivalry is generally condemned as a source of weakness, but there is ample evidence to the contrary. Stirred to active campaigning by the rivalry, unions enlist hitherto unorganized workers and keep their officers alert to the needs of their members.[2]

In terms of the security it enjoys, American unionism appears to be somewhere between French and Italian unionism on the one hand, and Low Country-British-Scandinavian unionism on the other, though much nearer the latter. Most American employers have resigned themselves to collective bargaining, though for many this attitude is of recent origin. But there is still a significant nonunion sector which could conceivably be used as a base for an antiunion offensive. And many employers who have been forced by law to deal with unions carry on virulent antiunion campaigns and would not hesitate to take advantage of any weakness in the position of their adversaries.

It may be, therefore, that a call for more rivalry would be premature. The lessons of history to which Leiserson appeals are not so simple and clear as he makes them out to be. There has scarcely been a period without union rivalry in the United States in the past century, but competition has often helped neither the unions nor the cause of democracy. The great expansion of unionism during the 1930's was due to a complex of factors much more complicated than mere rivalry between AFL and CIO. Had there been different organizational and personality relationships, a successful campaign might have been waged by a single federa-

---

[2] Leiserson, *op. cit.*, pp. 8–9.

tion. Nor can the recent decline in union dynamism be ascribed to the AFC–CIO merger, for a retardation of growth had set in years earlier.

The question of union rivalry in the United States is worthy of discussion, in spite of the difficulties which have been pointed out. It is likely to be far more effective than recent federal legislation in spurring internal democracy. Much of the force of the "right to work" argument will be removed if there is a greater degree of voluntarism. Nor should the possibility of rivalry be dismissed as an academic matter. Governmental policy can foster it, for example, by refusing recognition to the validity of no-raiding pacts. Even more important would be the questioning of the ethical basis of antidualism within the labor movement itself. There have always been strong divisive forces within American labor, and there is enough to be gained out of raiding to bring about considerable rivalry if the idea should once again become respectable, as it was when the AFL and CIO were vying with each other.

We must be under no illusion that the process would be costless, however. Intraplant relations might be less harmonious, and there is bound to be more industrial strife. Unions will have to be given greater immunity from employer attack, lest rivalry lead to a reversion to an open-shop pattern in which the worker has far fewer rights of self-determination than under the least democratic of trade unions.

INSTITUTIONS OF UNION GOVERNMENT

Most of the specific devices for the regulation of union government that we have examined are not necessarily conducive to greater worker welfare. The referendum, for example, has proved to be incompatible with the requirements of modern collective bargaining. About the method by which union officers are elected, Leiserson has pointed out with justification that "there is no evidence that union governments are more democratic as their officers are elected by one method or the other. The same undemocratic tendencies appear in the smaller number of organizations which elect by referendum as in the much greater number in which the convention chooses the executives."[3]

---

[3] Leiserson, *op. cit.*, pp. 218–219.

However, there are some European practices which are worth considering. One is the lay executive committee. Men who are earning their livelihood in the shop are not likely to be a match for professionals, but at the very least they can provide a direct line to rank-and-file sentiment. They may be more outspoken than career officials, and help break the one-man rule that is common to many unions. They are also more likely to look askance at the use of union funds for nonunion purposes.

The British system of the permanent general secretary has much to commend it. There are many organizations in the United States in which life tenure for leaders is common—large corporations, churches, universities, to name a few. This practice would hardly be likely to increase the average term of union office, and if there were in addition a compulsory retirement age, it might well reduce it. Permanence could conceivably lead to a greater toleration of minority factions within unions. The ostensible rationale for suppression of factionalism is that it tends to undermine the organization, but it is really the threat to the leadership that is feared. Even though the possibilities of successful revolt are slim, too much is at stake to take any chances. If the outcome of a factional victory were a change in union policy rather than in job holders, differences of opinion might be less suspect.

An American union practice which is consistently shocking to Europeans is the high earnings of union officials. These are often justified by the argument that in the absence of idealism or ideological motivation high salaries are essential if good men are to be attracted to the labor movement, that there is keen competition by industry for leadership talent, and that industrial salaries must be matched.

This argument does not stand up under examination. It would be difficult to prove that European labor leaders are less able than American, in spite of the fact that neither Socialist zeal nor high salaries are important in recruiting. There are many young, forceful, and obviously competent men to be found in the contemporary European labor movement. For the United States, one would scarcely want to argue that there is a direct relationship between the salary level and the ability and integrity displayed by union leadership; if anything, a good argument could be made for an inverse relationship.

The argument is sometimes posed in a different way. To the charge that American unions have modeled themselves too closely after the corporation, and adopted the ethics of the business world, the reply is made: would you rather have European-type unions? The implication is that European unions are radical bodies dedicated to the overthrow of capitalism, and that the choice is between business and revolutionary unionism.

To put the issue in this way is to misinterpret the European scene. None of the European trade unions which has gained security favors any revolutionary change in social or economic structure. All are staunchly anti-Communist, and have done a good job of fighting Communism without impairing civil liberties. Every movement has a program of social reform, but these are hardly more radical than the policies of many of the former CIO unions. Nationalization of industry has lost much of its appeal, and even advisory labor-management committees are not too popular. Revolutionary creeds are matters of ancient history, and have as little to do with current reality as the old AFL constitutional preamble had to do with the philosophy of that organization.[4]

The issue is whether a set of ethical values which permits a great income differential between trade union leaders and members, and which excuses undemocratic practices, can be justified by the argument that in the final analysis, the system promotes efficiency and economic well-being. There can be no question, for example, that American unions have been far more receptive to technological change than European unions, for all the talk of featherbedding. This is certainly a debatable issue, but our only concern here is to prevent misuse of the European analogy as an excuse for sidestepping it. What the European experience shows, if anything, is that it is possible for democratic trade unionism to be taken for granted as a matter of course, and that incorruptible union leadership can exist side by side with a business community whose ethics include the familiar paraphenalia of tax dodging and expense accounts.

TRADE UNIONS AND THE INDIVIDUAL

The right of the Swedish worker to bring to arbitration a dispute with his union—a different version of the United Automobile Workers' public review board—is worthy of study. Beyond that,

---

[4] The preamble read in part: "Whereas, a struggle is going on in all of the civilized world, between the oppressors and the oppressed of all countries, a struggle between the Capitalist and the Laborer, which grows in intensity from year to year, and will work disastrous results to the toiling millions, if they are not combined for mutual protection and benefit. . . ."

we have little to learn from the formal mechanism of the internal judicial process in European unions.

In protecting the individual against forced membership, we are in some ways ahead of Europe. Although closed or union shops are not provided by collective agreement in Great Britain or Scandinavia, "100 per cent unionism" prevails in many industries, and loss of employment and even further victimization of the nonunionist are by no means unknown. There is no equivalent of our safeguard of employment for the worker who has a disagreement with his union (under the Taft-Hartley Act). Mounting public concern and adverse court decisions are leading the British unions to reëxamine their positions. At the very least, conscientious objectors should be exempted from compulsory union membership; surely this is no more drastic than exempting them from military service in wartime.

There is not so much difference between American and European union political action as is commonly supposed. While American trade unions have been moving toward closer liaison with the Democratic party, European unions have been moving away from their traditional alliance with Socialist and Labor parties. Where collective affiliation is practiced, objecting individuals can escape the political levy by contracting out. In both Europe and the United States, dues money is used for partisan political purposes (except in United States federal elections, where political money must be collected voluntarily), but the practice is being increasingly questioned.

The Labor parties of Europe are undergoing intensive self-analysis, because it is clear that the old slogans and shibboleths have lost their appeal. If they are to attain, or retain, political power, it will have to be on the basis of a program which transcends the sectional interests of workers. There is going to be a reassessment of political-party–trade-union ties; although no political organization wants to cut itself off from a good source of funds, diminished dependence on the unions may be necessary to prevent alienation of the growing middle classes.

In both Europe and the United States, there is still plenty of room within the labor movement for improvement in the degree of tolerance which unpopular and unorthodox views are accorded. Many within the labor movement—as well as outside—have yet to realize that it is the diversity of opinion rather than the uniformity which is the strength of democratic institutions.

94

INDEX